D1280960

Hidden From History:
The Lives of Eight
American Women Scientists

AVISSON YOUNG ADULT SERIES

Hidden From History:
The Lives of Eight American Women Scientists

Kim K. Zach

Avisson Press, Inc.
Greensboro

119948

ISBN 1-888105-54-2
First edition
Printed in the USA

Library of Congress Cataloging-in-Publication Data

Zach, Kim K., 1958—
  Hidden from history: the lives of eight American women scientists / by Kim K. Zach.
    p. cm. — (Avisson young adult series)
  Summary: Short biographies of eight women who excelled in various scientific fields: Ellen Swallow Richards, Nettie Maria Stevens, Annie Jump Cannon, Alice Hamilton, Florence Sabin, Alice Catherine Evans, Grace Murray Hopper, and Gertrude Belle Elion.
  Includes bibliographical references and index. ISBN 1-888105-54-2 (pbk.)
  1. Women scientists — United States — Biography — Juvenile literature. [1. Scientists. 2. Women—Biography.] I. Title. II. Series.
Q141 .Z33 2002
509.2'273 —dc21
[B]

                                                      2002028151

Publisher's Note:
Efforts have been made to find the copyright holders of all photographs used in this book. If any person or organization believes they hold the copyright to a photograph herein, and have not been properly credited, please notify the publisher at the address above.

Contents

Introduction

*"Because women do not appear in
history or philosophy with anything like
the same prominence as men--the great names
that we know are but the accidental scraps."*
                                              --Walt Whitman

The National Women's Hall of Fame was established in 1969 as a way of honoring the contributions of American women in the arts, athletics, business, education, government, the humanities, philanthropy, and science. The Hall is located in Seneca Falls, New York, the birthplace of the women's rights movement.

The exhibits and artifacts on display pay tribute to some of the greatest women our country has produced. Over 150 women have been nominated and elected to the Hall for their roles in American history. But how many of these women have achieved the kind of prominence Walt Whitman speaks of?

When I first read through the National Women's Hall of Fame membership list, I realized what Whitman meant by "accidental scraps." I recognized only three names of the women who were scientists--Elizabeth Blackwell, Rachel Carson, and Maria Mitchell. I remember checking out biographies on each of them from the public library when I was in elementary school, but I don't recall hearing their names in the classroom.

As I scrolled through the list, the unfamiliar names intrigued me. Nettie Stevens proved that X and Y chromosomes determine sex. Alice Hamilton's research led to the first laws protecting the health and safety of American factory workers. Gertrude Elion won the Nobel Prize for developing drugs used in preventing organ transplant rejection and treating childhood leukemia.

As I read each woman's name and her achievements, I wondered, "Why haven't I heard of her before?" Their work has effected life-saving changes for people all over the world. But these women's names are absent from most science and American history curriculums and many reference books.

By contrast, the men of science we recognize is a long list, including Benjamin Franklin, Thomas Edison, Eli Whitney, Alexander Graham Bell, Jonas Salk, and Carl Sagan. Their accomplishments are highlighted in textbooks and encyclopedias. Their names are embedded in our popular culture and have a prominent place in our country's history.

Women have struggled for equality in many areas, but the field of science has been a particularly difficult one. Until the late nineteenth century, medical schools, laboratories, and hospitals were occupied by men.

Without education and opportunity, women did not have the means to begin scientific endeavors.

The situation began to change slowly as women's colleges were established and co-ed universities reluctantly admitted women. But even after earning their degrees, many women found the doors to employment firmly closed. When a job could be found at all, it usually meant less pay and fewer privileges than male co-workers.

The eight women scientists profiled in this book encountered obstacles simply because they were female. Though each woman's experience is uniquely her own, a few common threads run through each life story.

First, their families supported the idea of education for girls. A number of the eight women were educated at home during their early years. A majority of them had strong mothers who encouraged them, which was highly unusual for that time period. Second, nearly all of them were involved in teaching in some capacity, which is not at all surprising. Teaching was only one of two or three occupations women could engage in without raising the eyebrows of their neighbors. Some taught to earn money for their own education; others turned to teaching as the only employment open to them as scientists.

Finally, each woman faced prejudice with perseverance. In most cases there was a price to pay. This price involved not moving upward in her profession or gaining credit for her work. Yet each seemed willing to bypass promotion and recognition as long as she was able to do the work she loved. The work itself was of primary importance because it involved improving the quality of life for others.

A perfect example is Annie J. Cannon. She classified over 400,000 stars during her 40 years at the Harvard Observatory, but the information was published under a man's name as the *Henry Draper Catalogues.* Also consider Ellen Swallow Richards, the first female science student at MIT and the first female faculty member. She taught there for 40 years but was never given the title or benefits of "professor."

Their names and the names of countless other women of science need to be known as more than "accidental scraps." If their achievements do not become part of our recorded history, then we will have lost half of our American heritage.

— K.K.Z.

Chapter One

Ellen Swallow Richards
(1842-1911)
Chemist

*"The only trouble here is they won't let us study enough.
They are so afraid we shall break down, and you
know the reputation of the college is at stake, for the
question is, can girls get a college degree without
injuring their health."*
--from a letter to her mother while at Vassar

Dr. John Runkle, president of the Massachusetts Institute of Technology, looked across the long wooden table at the stunned faces of the men who sat on the school's admissions committee. He had just finished reading the application materials of Ellen Henrietta Swallow. No one spoke, but in the confused silence that followed, no words were necessary.

Each man knew what the other was thinking. A *woman* at MIT? Impossible.

The Institute was only five years old and the written by-laws were not complete. When MIT was established in 1865, no one had ever imagined the need to write a law that said, "Women need not apply." It was assumed that no woman ever would.

However, Ellen's application arrived with recommendations from Maria Mitchell, the famed astronomer, and A. C. Farrar, a Vassar professor of applied science. Dr. Runkle highly respected their opinions. He urged the committee to admit Ellen.

Reluctantly, the committe voted to allow her enrollment as a special student. Oddly enough, they also decided to charge Ellen no tuition or fees. Too ecstatic to ask the reason, Ellen was humbled by the offer. She vowed to measure up to the honor of being the first woman admitted to a scientific institution in the United States.

"I have the chance to do something no one else ever did," she wrote. "I hope that I am winning a way which others will keep open."

Only later did Ellen discover why she was not charged tuition or her name added to class lists. It was not for her benefit but for the protection of the school. If anyone protested her presence, MIT was prepared to claim she wasn't really a student. Outraged by the deception, Ellen said she would not have accepted the committe's offer had she known what lay behind it.

Following her graduation from MIT, Ellen used her skills as a chemist to show people how to establish a healthful, safe home by using scientific principles. And as one of the first environmental scientists, Ellen was a champion of pure water, clean air, and uncontaminated food. Today, she is recognized as both the founder of home economics and the creator of the branch of science called ecology.

~~~~~~~~~~~~~~~~~~~

Ellen Swallow Richards was born on December 3, 1842 on a small farm in Massachusetts. She was home schooled when it was uncommon for girls or boys to be educated beyond eighth grade. Luckily, her parents were both former schoolteachers.

Unhappy with the limited public school curriculum of the day, Peter and Fanny Swallow took their daughter's early years of education into their capable hands. They also disagreed with the common belief that girls' minds were inferior and educating them beyond basic domestic skills was useless, even unhealthy.

Ellen did learn to sew, bake, cook, and clean, but not just because she was a girl. Besides being useful, these skills taught her to coordinate hand and mind. Baking a prize-winning pie crust and understanding the properties of yeast and baking soda were an introduction to chemistry. Years later, when she was a student at Vassar, she wrote what a professor told his class: ". . . the profession of an analytical chemist is very profitable and means very nice and delicate work, fitted for ladies' hands."

Ellen eagerly absorbed these early lessons, as well as her letters and numbers. Later, she studied mathematics, logic, history, and literature. Ellen especially loved books and spent most of her spare time reading and discussing with her parents. She loved reading so much that she developed the ability to perform other tasks while she read.

Her parents also made certain that her education extended beyond the homemade classroom. Ellen learned botany from the garden she kept and biology from the animals they raised. She helped her father with the farm chores, too, in spite of having inherited her mother's tendency towards physical frailness.

A doctor's prescription of fresh air and sunshine eventually improved her health. In the meadows and along the brook behind their farmhouse, Ellen observed the ways of nature and environment. These childhood experiences laid the foundation of her life-long mission to examine the impact of clean air and pure water on people's health. They also formed her opinions about educational theories and how children should be taught.

Later in her life, she said: "What we do to kill learning! We put young children on hard seats, in cramped positions, force their heads into a dead book . . . [Instead] place the child in an environment rich in suggestion . . . furnish the [natural] materials for discovery . . . [he] needs pleasant surroundings--color, form, flowers, music--to express his ideas and to stimulate imaginative thoughts . . . to become master of his environment."

Leaving the Farm

By the age of 16, Ellen's thirst for learning had absorbed all her parents could teach her. Peter Swallow moved the family to Westford, Massachusetts, so that Ellen could attend Westford Academy, a high school which accepted female students. There she studied the classics under the direction of several headmasters who were young Harvard graduates. Ellen did so well that soon she was tutoring other students, especially in Latin and mathematics.

Ellen's father bought a small grocery store and, when she wasn't in school or caring for her ill mother, Ellen did the accounting, inventoried and ordered supplies, and waited on customers. As busy as she was, Ellen was never very far from a book. A familiar sight was Ellen near the stove reading or an open book on the counter, laid aside for the moment to wait on a customer.

Battling Depression

After graduating from high school, Ellen accepted a teaching position close to home. She continued to care for her mother and help in the store, but the workload was too great. Her first loyalty was to her parents, so she taught for only one year.

After her mother's health improved, Ellen took a daring step for a young, unmarried girl. She moved alone to the larger city of Worcester to attend school and teach. Ellen enjoyed the challenge of living by her own means, though it meant not eating much more than bread and milk. However, she was forced to return home when her mother fell ill again.

Without the stimulation of teaching, which she had loved, and having experienced independence, Swallow battled depression. She wanted to go on learning, but there was no one to teach her. Frustrated, Ellen said, "I was thwarted and hedged in on every side." In 1865, she read about the opening of Vassar College for women.

Ellen desperately wanted to go there, but she didn't have the $300 tuition. For the next two and a half years, she worked to save the money she needed to apply. She hired herself out as a tutor, cook, housekeeper, and nurse. Ellen described the waiting as "two years in purgatory."

Opportunity at Vassar

At age 26, Ellen was finally admitted to Vassar, entering as a junior because she had placed well on the entrance exam. Vassar was an experimental college opened in 1865 by beer entrepreneur Matthew Vassar as a favor to his niece.

People were shocked by a women's college. "Their nervous systems will not adapt to higher learning," they said. "They are too frail and delicate." Some of them wanted to believe the worst about the women who attended because they felt no real lady would consider higher education.

The faculty and students knew they were under scrutiny and that if they failed, it would be a step backward for all women. They were driven to disprove the ridiculous notions that learning "beyond their needs" was improper and unhealthy. In a letter home, Ellen wrote, "Much responsibility is thrown on us for the reputation of the college...no other institution can show whole classes of such hard workers."

Ellen developed an interest in science under the tutelage of two professors: astronomer Maria Mitchell and A.C. Farrar, who introduced her to applied chemistry. Ellen excelled in both subjects, although when she graduated two years later with a B.S. she said, "I've quite made up my mind to try chemistry for a life's study."

While she was intrigued by the stars, Ellen also recognized the intangible nature of astronomy. Chemistry was more suited to her belief in the practical applications of science, something she had been learning since her early education on the farm. Ellen's love for the outdoors had gradually overshadowed her love for books. Ellen brought everything she could from the outdoors into her laboratory---fossils, rocks, plants, and water. Under the lens of her microscope, Ellen observed her environment in its many forms.

Ellen was convinced that through chemistry, the environment could be made safer and improve people's quality of life. This, she decided, would be how she could make a difference in the world. But Ellen soon discovered a job in a chemistry laboratory just didn't exist for a woman in 1870.

She wrote letters of application to chemical firms in Dayton, Philadelphia, and Boston. All replied that they did not hire women. The social constraints of the day hadn't stopped her from getting an education, but it appeared they might stop her from using it.

In the face of rejection, Ellen remained optimistic. She wrote in her diary, "[I] have been trying to find suitable opportunity to attempt it, but everything seems to stop short at a blank wall. I trust something will come to pass."

That something was a suggestion by one of the chemical firms who had turned her down. Why not apply to the Massachusetts Institute of Technology? MIT had been established the same year as Vassar and quickly became well-known for its applied science courses. It did seem the ideal place for Ellen.

A First for MIT

After beginning her studies at MIT, Ellen so distinguished herself as a student that when Professor William Nichols needed an assistant for a water-sewage study assigned by the Massachusetts Board of Health, he chose her.

Nichols had been a part of a group of people at MIT who had originally been against admitting women. Of her assignment, Ellen wrote, "A new work has been put in my hands...by a professor who does not believe in women's education."

Nichols left Ellen in charge of the actual testing while he traveled to Europe to study water-analysis techniques there. It was she who observed the sewage, streams, and water supply of Massachusetts through her microscope and test tubes, looking for pollution and other impurities.

When Nichols made his report to the state legislature, he gave her the credit. "Most of the analytical work has been performed by Miss Ellen Swallow...I take pleasure in acknowledging my indebtedness to her valuable assistance by expressing my confidence in the accuracy of the results obtained."

The water study was significant for two reasons. First, it established the first state standards for water purity. Later studies relied on the initial test data so painstakingly gathered and recorded by Ellen. Second, whether or not MIT or other people were ready to acknowledge it, Ellen had become an international expert in water analysis.

When Ellen graduated in 1873 with a B.S. in chemistry, she was MIT's first female graduate and the first woman in America to earn a chemistry degree. That same year she was awarded an M.A. from Vassar based on her discovery of the metal vanadium through her work in chemical analysis of minerals.

Her Home as a Laboratory

Robert H. Richards, an MIT professor of mineralogy, came to admire Ellen's academic abilities and fell in love with her. Ellen thought she loved him, too, but she was afraid.

When Ellen had lived on her own in Worcester, she had observed the unhappiness that marriage brought many women. To a friend she had written, " . . .[what I saw] made me vow I would never bind myself with the chains of matrimony . . . girls don't get behind the scenes as I have, or they could not get up such an enthusiasm for the married life."

After two years of gentle persuasion, Robert convinced her that he did not expect her to give up her pursuit of a science career. Finally, she agreed to marry him.

Their marriage proved to be mutually beneficial. Both accomplished goals that could never have been reached without the other. Robert said, "She was of great assistance in my work...she took more than her share from the beginning." Ellen accompanied him on mineralogy excursions, including one which served as their honeymoon. She also translated and condensed the more than twenty papers that he received each week.

Marriage gave Ellen the financial stability she had never had, which enabled her to give her full concentration to science. Robert's connections also introduced her to people in the scientific community. He was never jealous of her accomplishments but always made certain to talk about her work to others and even wrote about it. He saved the reports, letters, and other papers documenting her contributions to science.

When they set up housekeeping in 1875, their home became an extension of Ellen's laboratory. She wrote, "The environment that people live in is the environment that they learn to live in, respond to, and perpetuate. If the environment is good, so be it. But if it is poor, so is the quality of life within it."

Ellen's belief in healthful living and safe environments led her to remodel the house, including replacing lead water pipes, installing a gas stove, and using scatter rugs instead of room-size carpeting. Ellen cooked simple, nutritious meals using energy-efficient methods. She and Robert also designed and installed a mechanical system for ventilating and circulating air.

A visitor to the Richards' home observed, "It was like breathing cleaner air to come into the house. The dust of non-essentials had been swept away and the supply of oxygen seemed greater here than elsewhere . . . at once restful and invigorating."

The Woman's Laboratory

In 1876, Swallow received permission to set up a

chemistry laboratory for female students at MIT. It was the first such laboratory of its kind in the world because its specific purpose was to encourage women to pursue scientific study. Many of the students were teachers who returned to their schools to set up laboratories and science curriculum where there had been none.

Working in a run-down garage behind the school, Ellen was professor, janitor, and fund-raiser for the equipment she needed. She received no salary or other monetary support from MIT. After two years, the school tore down the building and erected a new chemistry laboratory, one which allowed students of any sex to study there.

During this time, Ellen had also been studying herself for a Ph.D. Even though she had completed all of the necessary coursework, MIT would not award her the advanced degree. The department heads, who were men, refused to allow a woman to be the first person to receive a doctorate degree in chemistry.

Ellen's husband later said, "She wanted a Doctor's Degree more than anything else, but she had to give up the idea, one of her greatest disappointments in life."

Working for Public Health

In 1884, Ellen finally received a salaried position on the MIT faculty as an instructor in the new discipline of sanitary chemistry. She taught courses in the analysis of food, water, sewage, and air.

Beginning in 1878, she was hired by industry as an analytical chemist. She tested air, oils, minerals, and water. She also tested foods, particularly grocery staples like sugar and milk, for adulteration by storekeepers. There were no laws at that time against shopkeepers for adding sand to the sugar they sold or yellow dyes to their milk.

The Massachusetts Board of Health proposed to do the first statewide study of water pollution in the country. They approached an MIT professor named Dr. Drown to head the study and he wanted Swallow to be his assistant. Together they analyzed over 40,000 samples from Massachusetts' streams, water supplies, and sewage systems. The result was a National Chlorine Map, which set the standard for later sanitary surveys.

The Boston Board of Education asked her to create a school hot lunch program. It succeeded in providing hot, nutritious meals to students who had previously been eating cake and candy. The program was a model for similar programs throughout the country.

By the mid-1880's, she was one of the top chemists in the country, consulted by corporations, schools, mine owners, and insurance companies.

Paving the Way for Home Economics

Around 1890, Ellen's focus shifted to the field of home economics, which she first termed "human ecology." She opened the New England kitchen to help Boston immigrants learn about nutrition and it served as a model for Jane Addams' Hull House.

When the U.S. Department of Agriculture began to issue nutrition bulletins, she was asked to be a consultant for the project. A school of housekeeping that she helped organize at the Woman's Educational and

Industrial Union in Boston was later incorporated into the department of home economics when Simmons College was founded. In 1899, she set up a summer conference in Lake Placid, New York to organize the field of home economics. This included planning courses of study for public schools and colleges and setting standards for teacher certification.

In 1908, the American Home Economics Association was founded and she served as president of the organization until 1910. She created the *Journal of Home Economics,* the association's publication, and used her own money to establish it.

Ellen published about twenty books and manuals related to her work. These include *The Chemistry of Cooking and Cleaning* (1882), *Home Sanitation: A Manual for Housekeepers* (1887), *Air, Water, and Food for Colleges* (1900), and *Laboratory Notes on Industrial Water Analysis: A Survey Course for Engineers* (1908).

The Human Link to the Environment

Through her extensive studies, Ellen confirmed that people became ill if they were exposed to contaminated air, water, food, and soil. Her books, lectures, and teaching methods educated people about their right to know what they were eating, breathing, and drinking.

In an MIT convocation speech, she wrote, "The quality of life depends on the ability of society to teach its members how to live in harmony with their environment-- defined first as the family, then with the community, then with the world and its resources."

Ellen spent her life trying to bridge the gap created

by prejudice against women in education, especially in science. Along the way, she increased people's awareness of the environment and healthy living, while founding two branches of science, ecology and home economics. Incredibly, she foresaw the 20th century problems of energy depletion and air pollution and warned people to take action.

Less than a month before her death in 1911 at age sixty-eight, Ellen Swallow Richards was still actively traveling and giving speeches about her ideas. As a woman to whom others had tried to deny an education, she realized that information had life-altering potential. She said, "In an age when environment is changing, we must give knowledge greater distribution, even reorganization, to restore the human link to environment."

(Courtesy Carnegie Institution of Washington)

Chapter Two

Nettie Maria Stevens
(1861-1912)
Biologist/Geneticist

"How could you think your questions would bother me?
They never will, so long as I keep my enthusiasm for
biology; and that, I hope, will be as long as I live."
--from a letter to a former student

A quiet evening calm had settled over the buildings on the Bryn Mawr college campus. Hallways and classrooms were dark and empty, with the exception of a biology workroom. There Nettie Stevens leaned over a microscope perched near the edge of a black laboratory table. On the slide beneath the powerful lens of the microscope lay a scene which had captivated her thousands of times before. Tiny fertilized cells were busily dividing. Nettie was still watching them, still wondering.

The year was 1905 and Nettie was close to reaching the conclusion which would completely change the way scientists and lay people viewed the conception and birth of a baby. Before then, most people commonly believed that the sex of a child was determined by the mother, and perhaps also influenced by environmental factors.

Nettie disproved this long-held notion when she uncovered with her microscope and sound reasoning what had been hidden for so long. The gender of a baby depends on which type of sperm cell fertilizes the egg. One with an X chromosome produces a girl and one with a Y chromosome produces a boy.

She was the first scientist to put her findings in writing and state her conclusions with conviction. Her theory was initially rejected. Then as it gained acceptance, credit was given to a male researcher who had been her teacher and colleague.

Almost a century later, the scientific community is just now beginning to acknowledge Nettie's contribution.

~~~~~~~~~~~~~~~~~~~~~~~

Nettie was born in rural Vermont in 1861 to fifth-generation New Englanders. Her father Ephraim Stevens supported his family, which included another daughter Emma and wife Julia, by work as a handyman and carpenter. Julia died when Nettie was only a toddler. Mr. Stevens remarried two years later, so the girls had a mother figure as they grew up.

When Nettie and her sister were of school age, the family moved to Westford, Massachusetts. They attended a public elementary school and then high school at Westford Academy. Nettie displayed an enthusiasm for learning and was especially interested in mathematics. She was a top student in all her classes including English, writing, logic, Greek and Latin, music, and geography.

Nettie graduated in 1880 with as much education as a girl could hope to obtain during the post-Civil War days. It was expected that she would use that education to earn money to help her family until she found a husband. With her career options limited to teaching, nursing, or housekeeping, Nettie chose teaching.

She found a position at a high school in New Hampshire, teaching the same courses in which she had excelled only a year earlier. While Nettie soon realized that she could never be satisfied spending her life as a teacher, it did serve two purposes. First, teaching was a daily reminder of her thirst for learning. Second, it was a way to earn money to continue her own education.

Getting a College Education

After three terms, Nettie had managed to save enough of her salary to attend a teacher's college, Westfield Normal School, in Westfield, Massachusetts. Her record there was spotless. In her class of 30, she merited the highest scores in the entrance exams and perfect grades in geometry, chemistry, and algebra. She completed the four-year program in only two years and graduated as the top student.

Nettie didn't record her first glimpse of the tiny world that appeared beneath the lens of a microscope. More than likely it was during one of her laboratory classes at Westfield. Certainly her interest in science was piqued by what she observed. Combined with her natural curiosity, Nettie's skill in using the microscope nudged her to focus on the biological sciences.

She completed the requirements for a teaching certificate in 1883. That was not enough education to satisfy her. Nettie wanted to do graduate work and earn a master's degree, but that would be impossible until she had earned a bachelor's degree. The same obstacle once again stood in her way--lack of money. So Nettie returned to teaching.

Back at Westford Academy

For the next several years, Nettie's own pursuit of education was delayed but her dreams were not abandoned. She obtained a teaching position at her old high school, Westford Academy in 1884. Nettie was creative and enthusiastic in the classroom, especially when teaching any science course. No doubt she introduced her students to the mysteries of microscopic plants and animals. Along with her teaching, she set a course of self-study so that she would be well-prepared when the opportunity for college arrived.

Nettie also served as Westford's librarian. Later she was an assistant principal at a school in another Massachusetts town. Performing all of her duties in a fair and efficient manner, she was well-liked by hundreds of students and colleagues alike.

What patience she must have possessed to help so many with their educations while looking forward to the time when she could continue her own. By 1896, Nettie had saved enough money to go back to college. It had taken thirteen years.

Earning Advanced Degrees

Even though she now had the financial means to attend college, Nettie faced another roadblock. She was thirty-five years old and had last been a student more than a decade before.

Stanford University in California was willing to gamble by letting her into their program. The university was gaining a reputation for opening its doors to women. However, they admitted Nettie on probationary status. She would have to prove herself academically before she could be considered a regular student.

After only a few months, her professors realized that Nettie was not only one of the brightest students at the university but one of the most self-motivated. Her years of teaching high school science and self-study had given her a firm foundation in scientific principles. She was soon transferred to the regular program.

Nettie earned her Bachelor's degree by 1899 and her Master's degree one year later. Most of her work for the two degrees was completed under the tutelage of Professor Frank Mace McFarland. She was his research assistant for four summers at an oceanside laboratory in Pacific Grove, California, studying microscopic plant and animal life.

Her master's degree thesis, titled "Studies on Ciliate Infusoria," was about protozoan life cycles. The thesis was later the basis for her first published scientific paper.

With her master's degree in hand, Nettie was determined to keep studying. This time she set her sights on a Ph.D. She left California and enrolled at Bryn Mawr College in Pennsylvania.

Post-graduate Research in Europe

Bryn Mawr was established in 1880 as a college for women. Nettie studied under two prominent biologists of the time, Edmund Beecher Wilson and Thomas Hunt Morgan. After only one year, Nettie had distinguished herself as an excellent student.

Professor Morgan was influential in helping her win a pair of fellowships for study in Europe. Nettie was excited about the opportunity to learn from several world-famous geneticists. Nettie first studied at the Zoological Station in Naples, Italy. Then she went to the Zoological Institute at Wurzburg, Germany.

There Nettie laid the groundwork for her X-Y chromosome theory. Chromosomes, tiny structures present in all cells, were thought to play a part in characteristics inherited by living things.

After two wonderful years, Nettie returned to the United States. She had earned a reputation as a superb microscopist and tireless researcher by the time she was awarded her Ph.D. in 1903 from Bryn Mawr. At forty-two years old, she had achieved a level of education beyond what most women and many men had not.

But once again, Nettie wasn't content. She was already looking ahead to her next goal.

A Research Grant from the Carnegie Institute

Nettie wanted to devote the rest of her life to genetic research. This would not be possible unless she had some measure of financial independence. Nettie could go back to teaching high school science, yet here was the dilemma. She would have the money but not the time to do the research she loved.

When Nettie found out that several research assistant ships were available through the Carnegie Institute of Washington, D.C., she completed an application. Both Professors Wilson and Morgan sent letters to the Institute, highly recommending her. They cited her self-reliance and intellectual abilities which made her one of the finest researchers they knew.

Wilson and Morgan also claimed that her work was equal to any man with the same level of education. For this time period, it was quite a recommendation and highly unusual.

Nettie waited nervously for months for a reply. Meanwhile, Bryn Mawr had given her a one-semester research fellowship which provided a brief reprieve. She worked with Professor Morgan in his study of the chromosomal behavior of small insects called aphids. Nettie was glad for the experience but still worried. If her application with Carnegie was turned down, she felt that her career as a research scientist would be over.

Fortunately, in 1904, she finally received word. The Carnegie Institute had awarded her one of their grants. Nettie was about to embark on the research that led to one of the most important biological discoveries in the history of genetics.

The "Accessory Chromosome" Theory

Without financial worries, Nettie was free to

conduct research of her own design. She decided to base her studies on the meal worm, the worm-like larva of a beetle which commonly infests bakeries and granaries.

By examining the sex cells of these tiny insects with her microscope, Nettie eventually observed a distinctive difference between the male and female cells. She noted that an unfertilized egg always contained two of the larger X chromosomes. However, sperm cells were of two types. These sex cells carried either one large X chromosome or one smaller Y chromosome.

Nettie reached the conclusion that a female resulted when an egg was fertilized by a sperm cell carrying an X-chromosome. A male was produced when a Y-carrying sperm cell fertilized the egg. This theory was fairly radical, as it contradicted everything medical scientists and lay people had believed for centuries about how sex is determined.

Although Nettie believed strongly in what her own eyes and deductive reasoning told her, she knew others would receive her discovery with skepticism. Long-held scientific beliefs are difficult to reverse.

How many women throughout history have suffered blame for their failure to produce a male heir? Now here was a theory, being promoted by a woman, which said that if a daughter appeared rather than a son, it was the father's "fault."

None of these potential biases prevented Nettie from courageously making her theory public. She reported her findings in a paper titled, "Studies in Spermatogenesis, with Especial Reference to the 'Accessory Chromosome'." She submitted the paper to the Carnegie Institute as required by the grant. They published it.

Wilson Receives Credit for the X-Y Theory

While Nettie's research project was in progress, former Bryn Mawr professor Edmund B. Wilson was researching the same subject. Wilson came to an almost identical conclusion. Ironically, he sat on the advisory committee which reviewed Nettie's paper. Even more amazing is the fact that his paper was dated May 5, 1905, less than three weeks before Nettie's paper, dated May 23, 1905.

Although historians now say that Wilson and Nettie, his former student, drew the same conclusion independently, in a sense, they reached the conclusion as a team. Each was aware of the genetic research that the other was doing. Both had even referred to each other's work in their individual research notes.

Wilson did not try to claim sole credit for the discovery, although it is generally attributed to him. Some historians believe this was because his career had already been established when Nettie was getting started. His paper had also been published before hers, and of course, he was a man.

Acceptance of the "Accessory Chromosome" Theory

The main difference between the two researchers' findings was the degree to which they claimed the X and Y chromosomes affected sex differences. While Wilson gave some leeway to environmental factors, Nettie stated in no uncertain terms that chromosomes were the sole determiners of sex.

Wilson finally concurred completely with her when he published his second paper in October 1905. But it took nearly five years until her theory was generally accepted by other scientists. Even Professor Morgan, who had helped further her career in research, doubted her findings. In 1906 he was still arguing that factors like egg size were an influence and that sex was not determined until after fertilization.

Morgan finally conceded to the theory in 1910. But by this time, it was Wilson's name that was attached to the findings.

The Research Continues

Nettie went on with her research, largely ignoring the controversy. She didn't seem to be bothered by the fact that Wilson was receiving the recognition for their discovery. Nettie wanted neither fame nor fortune. Only her research mattered.

For the next seven years, she worked with aphids and more than 50 types of beetles. These studies verified that her original theory of sex determination had been correct.

From 1901 to 1912, Nettie published almost 40 papers, quite a large number considering her brief career. She received the Ellen Richards Prize for her paper about the life cycle of aphids. Worth $1,000, the award enabled her to return to the Zoological Station in Naples, Italy for more study.

Nettie also spent time as a researcher in New York

at the Cold Spring Harbor biological laboratory. In 1908 and 1909 she again studied at the University of Wurzburg in Germany.

During these final years, Nettie was a professor at Bryn Mawr. She brought to the college classroom the same qualities that had made her a beloved high school teacher. Countless students were inspired to enter careers in science through her cultivation of the love of scientific research. Nettie had a particular microscope at the Bryn Mawr laboratory that was her favorite and it was dubbed "the Nettie Maria."

Just as Nettie was hitting her stride as a researcher and teacher, she was diagnosed with breast cancer. She sought treatment at Johns Hopkins Hospital in Baltimore but the disease was at an advanced stage. Nettie died at the hospital on May 4, 1912.

If Nettie Stevens' research career had not been cut short, what other contributions to science might she have made?

Following her death, Professor Morgan paid tribute to Nettie by writing, "...Miss Stevens had a share in a discovery of importance and her name will be remembered for this... ." But somehow her name was lost.

Chapter Three

Annie Jump Cannon
(1863-1941)
Astronomer

*" In these days of great trouble and unrest, it is good to
have something outside our own planet, something fine
and distant....Let people look to the stars for comfort"*
—From an interview during World War II

Annie Jump Cannon reached for her mother's hand as
she clambered up the ladder through the narrow trapdoor.
From the roof of the family home, the Delaware sky at
night arched over them like a brilliant canopy. Following
her mother's finger as it traced the constellations, Annie
eagerly sought the already familiar shapes.

In the small attic room below, she and her mother
had studied the names and positions of many stars. By
candlelight Annie sat in her mother's lap and turned the
pages of an old astronomy textbook. When her hand could
grip a pencil, she sketched crude but detailed maps of
what she had seen.

The time the two shared together in their
makeshift observatory was the beginning of Annie's life-

long fascination with the stars. She spent the rest of her life studying and observing the heavens.

Her achievements at Harvard were legendary and she became known as "the dean of women astronomers." Annie refined the system of spectral classification which remains in use today. Only a few modifications to the system were made in 1998.

She also identified and classified more stars than any other astronomer in the world. Her findings were assembled and published in nine volumes known as the *Henry Draper Catalogues*. They represented the sum of her life's work, yet they carried not her name, but the name of a Harvard-approved man. However, Annie refused to make an issue of this fact.

Annie's international reputation as an expert in her field disproved the notion that a woman's intellect was inferior and that her health would be compromised by using it. Thanks to the early influence of her mother, she became one of the most well-known female astronomers of the early 20th century.

Her belief in the value of her work was expressed when she wrote, "Classifying the stars has helped in all studies of the structure of the universe. No greater problem is presented to the human mind. Teaching man his relatively small sphere in the creation, it also encourages by its lessons of the unity of Nature and shows him that his power of comprehension allies him with the great intelligence over-reaching all."

When Mary Elizabeth Cannon married Annie's father, Wilson Lee Cannon, she inherited four children from his first marriage. She gave birth to three children of her own- Annie, on December 11, 1863, and then two more daughters.

Annie's mother was the quiet force behind her success in the classroom. At Dover Academy Annie did well in all subjects, but particularly math. She had a photographic memory and a nimble mind kept her at the head of the class.

Annie graduated at age 16. When her teachers approached Annie's father about college for the girl, he readily agreed.

Unlike many husbands and fathers of his time, Wilson Cannon was proud of the intelligence displayed by both his wife and daughter. As a wealthy shipbuilder and politician, he could afford to send Annie to any of the best colleges. He selected Wellesley, only five years old, but a college that had already established itself as a leading academic institution for women.

He believed that Annie could earn a college degree and still be young enough to marry a suitable husband when she returned.

Learning Physics and Astronomy

Annie was determined to take advantage of the opportunity of going to college, which she knew was not available to very many young women in 1880. The possibilities for her life became apparent when she studied physics and astronomy under Sarah F. Whiting. Whiting was both a role model and mentor for the young women she taught.

Whiting was knowledgeable about the latest scientific techniques and equipment and she made sure her students had access to both. Her energy and enthusiasm were contagious and she quickly became Annie's favorite teacher.

Although Whiting was technically a professor of physics, she organized the first astronomy classes after a visit to the Harvard Observatory. Wellesley didn't build its own observatory until 1900. In the meantime, Annie and the other students learned astronomy without one. From a college balcony, they watched the great comet of 1882 pass overhead through the lens of a 4-inch Browning telescope.

Whiting also learned from a visit to Harvard about a new instrument called a spectroscope. Of course, she made certain that Wellesley soon owned one.

Annie's attraction to the spectroscope was inevitable. While she studied physics by day, she was drawn to the laboratory at night with its promise of viewing her beloved stars. She was among the first students to master the useful new tool.

A spectroscope contained a prism that, when starlight passed through it, separated the light into bands of different colors and lengths. This spectrum was then broken down into a pattern of lines and bands, which astronomers could use to study and identify stars, since each star had its own pattern. This pattern is comparable to a person's fingerprint or the product bar codes scanned by computers today.

Annie spent countless hours with the spectroscope, examining individual stars and recording her observations. This early work inspired her interest in classifying stars, the area in which she established a career in astronomy a decade later.

But her first year at Wellesley was not without struggle. The biting New England winter left her with a succession of colds and ear infections from which recovery was slow. She suffered from a slight hearing loss, which grew progressively worse, eventually resulting in complete deafness.

Annie refused to mark her deafness as a handicap. Undaunted, she reasoned that an astronomer did not need a sense of hearing anyway. The things one did need-sharp eyes, attention to detail, ability to concentrate-she already possessed. They were skills whose seeds had been planted and nurtured by her mother.

A Decade in Delaware

Annie graduated with a B.S. in physics in 1884 and returned to Delaware high society but the transition was uncomfortable. Many of the girls she had known were married and some had become mothers. Of the single women left, she found herself at age 21 to be not only the oldest, but the most educated. Even though Annie was an attractive girl, she stood out as being different and her inability to hear made some social engagements uneasy experiences.

Frustration with her predicament overwhelmed her. Annie felt she had taken an enormous step backwards. She had gone from four years of immersion in a world which she found intellectually stimulating to spending her days helping her mother with household duties, reading, cooking, and playing the piano.

Wilson Cannon had been quite mistaken in thinking that Annie could abandon her interest in astronomy and be satisfied with marriage. Annie had no interest in getting married or working at a job which society deemed proper for an unmarried lady. Annie felt useless, with so much free time and no productive outlet for her scientific knowledge.

A trip to Europe in 1892 only increased her restlessness. Annie loved the freedom of traveling and became a photography buff when she recorded her trip using one of the newly-invented box cameras. She compiled the photos and descriptive text into a booklet. It was published and sold as a souvenir at the Chicago World Fair in 1893.

Annie wrote in her journal, "I am sometimes very dissatisfied with my life here. I do want to accomplish something so badly. There are so many things that I could do if I only had the money. And when I think that I might be teaching and making money, and still all the time improving myself , it makes me feel unhappy and as if I were not doing all I can."

When Annie's mother died a short time later, the situation worsened. Without her mother's companionship and encouragement, living in the house where she grew up became intolerable. In desperation, she wrote to Sarah Whiting, nearly begging for a job in the physics department.

One of Pickering's Women

Whiting responded immediately, offering Annie a job as her assistant. After ten years away, Annie eagerly and gratefully went back to Wellesley. She also enrolled as a special student of astronomy at nearby Radcliffe, Harvard's college for women, because they were allowed to study at the Harvard Observatory.

Annie's work there caught the attention of observatory director Edward C.Pickering. Her previous experience with both photography and spectroscopy led him to hire her to assist in an extensive project he was initiating.

Pickering's goal was to classify and catalogue all the stars down to the ninth magnitude, which is about sixteen times fainter than the human eye can see. The advent of photography made this possible. Scientists were able to take photographs of the stars, so they could be studied at any time, with no more waiting for nighttime or clear skies.

At the age of 34, Annie had her first official job as an astronomer. She was part of a team led by a Scottish woman named Williamina Fleming who had once worked as Pickering's maid. Pickering had hired Fleming on a whim after an incident with an incompetent male assistant. Her success convinced Pickering that women were ideally suited to the requirements of astronomy because they were more observant and patient than men.

Annie's role was to examine the photographic plates (called spectrograms) with a magnifying glass. First, she identified each star in the picture according to its spectrum.

The bars and lines told her trained eye various things about each star, such as its composition, temperature, speed, and size. Then she classified each star by putting it in a group with similar stars. She used the system developed by Fleming, utilizing twenty-two categories.

Annie and Fleming shared similar qualities, which set them apart from other assistants. As a result, both enjoyed greater independence and status at the Harvard Observatory. When Fleming died in 1911, it seemed natural for Annie to carry on the work that Fleming had begun.

Census Taker of the Stars

That same year Annie was appointed curator of the Harvard Observatory. The fragile glass plates which held the first-ever photographic mapping of the sky were now her responsibility.

She continued identifying and classifying stars for Pickering, but she was on her own without Fleming's guiding hand. Both jobs must have seemed burdensome at first, but Annie lost herself in the stars and became absorbed by the sheer enormity of the task.
It was a time-consuming job, requiring patience and discipline.

To an untrained eye, the spectrograms looked only like odd streaks of light, but Annie remarked, "They aren't just streaks to me. Each spectrum is the gateway to a wonderful world."

Eventually Annie grew so adept at inspecting the

glass plates, each bearing the images of hundreds of spectra, that she averaged three stars per minute.

As a result, between 1911 and 1915, Annie classified stars at the rate of 5,000 per month and 225,300 stellar spectra in all, twenty times the number Fleming had classified.

The Harvard System of Spectral Classification

At first Annie continued to use Fleming's classification system, which labeled the different groups in order from A to Q. But Annie was working at a phenomenal rate, identifying stars that had never been classified before. Feeling slightly disloyal, she discovered that Fleming's system was inadequate. Some categories had only a few stars in them or none at all and some of Annie's new stars didn't fit into the existing categories.

Annie refined the system when she developed a method to classify stars by their surface temperature. She found that different temperatures caused distinctive differences within the star spectra. Using letters, she arranged the categories to rank the stars from hottest (blue and white), hot (yellow), cool (orange), and coolest (red).

The new letter sequence she implemented was OBAFGAKM, which some later student of astronomy, trying to remember the order, devised the following sentence: Oh Be A Fine Girl And Kiss Me. This system was adopted by the International Astronomical Union in 1913 as the standard for stellar classification and is still in use today.

The Henry Draper Catalogues

In 1918, Harvard began the task of publishing Annie's findings as the *Henry Draper Catalogues*. They were named in honor of Henry Draper, a pioneer of astronomical photography, whose widow had funded Pickering's project.

The nine-volume project took longer than Pickering had estimated. The final volume wasn't completed until 1924. By this time, Annie was in her sixties and had been working as an astronomer for almost thirty years. In 1925 and 1949, two more volumes, known as the *Henry Draper Extension,* were published.

The Draper catalogues, sometimes called "the bible of modern astronomy," are still considered essential equipment in observatories all over the world. Besides being a treasury of information, the catalogues are also valued for their consistency, the result of one woman's long-term, steadfast work.

The Dean of Women Astronomers

In spite of her captivation with the stars, Annie chose not to live in scientific isolation. She loved entertaining in "Star Cottage," her house near the observatory. With a powerful hearing aid, she talked to famous scientists and students alike. She was an expert bridge player and was famous at Harvard for her oatmeal cookies.

Annie enjoyed traveling, not just for the adventure of seeing new places but of meeting new people. She actively supported the cause of women's suffrage and was a member of the National Women's Party.

During the last ten years of her life, Annie received numerous awards and honors. She was the first woman to win the Draper Gold Medal given by the National Academy of Science. She was also elected to membership in the Royal Astronomical Society of England, one of only six people since the society began in 1820. However, it was an honorary position only, since women weren't yet allowed to be full members.

She received the Ellen Richards Research Prize in 1932 from the Society to Aid Scientific Research by Women. Annie donated the cash prize to the American Astronomical Society to establish an award earmarked especially for women astronomers. Annie designed the award, which was later called the Annie Jump Cannon Prize, as a brooch rather than the usual medal as a courtesy to the women who would wear it.

A Lifetime of Star-gazing

In all, Annie classified more than 350,000 stars, the largest body of information ever accumulated by any individual or group in the field of astronomy. *The Henry Draper Catalogues* earned her recognition as one of the greatest experts in this field

She was the first woman ever to receive an honorary science degree from Oxford University. When the honor was bestowed, cited were her unequalled contributions to the new science of astrophysics.

In 1938, Annie was finally offered a permanent faculty position at Harvard. Unfortunately, this honor came rather late, as Annie lived only three more years.

However, as usual, the tangible reward itself meant little to her.

It was the relationship with her stars that mattered and she continued to labor over them until age 77. She was not ready to retire, but heart disease forced her to stop working. She died a short time later, on April 13, Easter Sunday, 1941.

Only a few months before her death, in a letter to a former Wellesley classmate, Annie wrote, "At the observatory, I am classifying, classifying, and now getting ready to start on a large piece for Yale Observatory. It will be a job! I keep several assistants busy doing minor details. Of course, I love to do it."

And that was Annie J. Cannon's secret. She possessed extraordinary powers of observation and an amazing memory, but the key to her longevity as an astronomer was the love she had for her work.

For almost eighty years, Annie watched the stars and she remained as dazzled by them as she had been when she first stood as a little girl on the rooftop. Her mother's delightful stories about the constellations never left her. They had endured, like the stars whose gentle light had been traveling towards the earth for millions of years.

Chapter Four

Alice Hamilton
(1869-1970)
Physician
Founder of Industrial Medicine

"All the accurately careful, elaborate work that I have been taught to consider is ignored here, and I am expected to make off-hand diagnoses, rapid prescriptions, and meet emergencies without losing my head. None of which I can do at all. There is no laboratory [and] the microscope is not as good as my own."
--written during her first year of internship

I want to become a doctor," said eighteen year old Alice Hamilton. She was standing in the parlor of her large, elegant family home in Fort Wayne, Indiana. Her parents and older sister Edith, seated before her, couldn't believe she was serious.

"A doctor? How unsuitable! Why not a career in

teaching, like Edith?" Women physicians were still a novelty in the late 1800's, even though Elizabeth Blackwell had paved the way forty years earlier and 4,500 women had since earned medical degrees. Shocked and dismayed, Alice's parents questioned her reasoning. Certainly it was not considered proper for young ladies from refined families to enter medicine. In addition, the Victorian code of the time made it taboo to even discuss the human body and its functions.

Although Alice had anticipated her family's reluctance to accept her decision, their reaction seemed to be at odds with the way she and her siblings had been reared.

First, their grandmother was a staunch advocate for women's rights. Also, Alice's mother Gertrude had always urged her daughters to speak their minds freely and to prepare for a career. She wanted them to experience the personal freedom she had never had and the chance to find a purpose in life.

Gertrude often talked to her girls about social injustices, too. "There are two kinds of people. The ones who say, 'Somebody ought to do something about it, but why should it be I' and those who say, "Somebody must do something about it, then why not I?" These words planted the seed of belief in Alice's mind that whatever career she chose, it should be one of service.

Alice felt that medicine would allow her to serve people and make a difference in their lives. She refused to become a teacher simply because it was an acceptable way for a woman to earn a living. So in spite of her family's objections, Alice finalized her plans for medical school.

It was the first step in a long career during which Alice pioneered the new science called industrial medicine. Through her efforts, workplaces were made safer from toxic substances through the passage of laws protecting the health of workers.

Alice received many honorary degrees and awards. Ironically, one of the most distinctive honors came in 1944. Her name was included among the many listings in the reference book *Men of Science*.

~~~~~~~~~~~~~~~~~

Alice was born on February 27, 1869 into a world of wealth and privilege. Her grandfather had been one of the founders of Fort Wayne and had amassed a fortune in business. She grew up happily playing with her three sisters and many cousins, who could roam freely about the acres of the family's estate.

Alice's parents were progressive-minded when it came to education. The children were taught at home because both parents disapproved of the public schools. Her father Montgomery thought the curriculum over-emphasized mathematics and American history, while her mother felt the hours were too long for children to be kept indoors.

Much of what the girls learned was from reading on their own, but they also studied history, literature, and languages -- Latin, French, and German. Alice and her sisters had free access to their father's large reference library. Once when Alice asked a question about physics, rather than answering, he pointed her towards the *Encyclopaedia Britannica.*

When Alice turned 17, she was sent to Miss Porter's, a boarding school in Connecticut. It was family tradition that female Hamiltons attend the school. The education she received there was neither rigorous (no tests or grades) nor substantial. Students could choose the subjects they wanted to study, so Alice of course chose languages and literature, subjects in which was already adept. She avoided math and science altogether.

Preparing for Medical School

Although Alice and her sisters had been raised in privileged circumstances in their home in Fort Wayne, Indiana, this changed while she was away at Miss Porter's. Her father lost his business and the family was forced to sell some of its real estate in order to pay debts. It was this situation that prompted Alice and Edith to seriously think of making their own living and, eventually, helping the family financially.

Edith chose to be a teacher and enrolled at Bryn Mawr, a women's college. In spite of the feelings of her family, Alice was determined to go to medical school. Unlike Edith, she shunned a traditional female career, explaining, " . . . as a doctor I could go anywhere I pleased--to far off lands or city slums--and be quite sure I could be of use anywhere. I should meet all sorts and conditions of men, I should not be tied down to a school or college as a teacher is, or have to work under a superior, as a nurse must do."

However, Alice had a lot of catching up to do

before she could even hope to be accepted at a medical school. With no background in science and little interest in the subject itself, she forged ahead with her studies. She was tutored by a high school teacher in physics and chemistry, and took anatomy at a small medical college in Fort Wayne.

After watching her work steadily for nearly four years, her father told her, "Alice, I am now convinced that you really want to study medicine. You must have the best medical education open to women."

Her father's change in attitude was a relief to Alice. It was one less worry in a huge undertaking. She vowed to remain deserving of his support.

Earning a Medical Degree

In 1890, at age 21, Alice was accepted at the University of Michigan Medical School in Ann Arbor. It was one of the top-rated medical schools in the country and one of the few whose doors were open to women. Even so, women had gained admission only twenty years before, and Alice's class numbered just thirteen women out of forty seven students.

Men and women sat together in the same lecture halls for all courses with one exception. Anatomy dissections took place, for the sake of modesty, in two separate rooms. And even though it was deemed unnecessary to separate students during anatomy lectures, men and women sat on opposite sides of the rooms, divided by a long strip of red paint. Alice gradually discovered that she did have an aptitude for science. She completed the work required of her, even the surgery rotation which she disliked intensely. But Alice loved working in the laboratory. Fascinated by what she observed through the lens of her microscope, she learned to recognize healthy human cells and the organs they came from. In her favorite class, pathology, she identified diseases by studying the changes they caused in once-healthy cells.

Alice delighted in solving the mysteries inherent in pathology. During her senior year, she was chosen to accompany one of the head doctors on his patient rounds. In the more complex cases, Alice took notes, performed laboratory tests, compiled the data, and made diagnoses. She was a medical detective, her beloved microscope a partner.

Alice didn't feel as comfortable examining patients as she did in the laboratory. After one of her clinical experiences, she wrote, "...we left him and went to examine his expectoration [under the microscope] to see if there were any tubercle bacilli . . . I was rejoicing over the little red lines that I had found until I remembered what it meant to the poor man; that sobered me. I don't mind chemicals or frogs even, or cats, but when it comes to living, feeling people, then I grow frightened."

Fear of hospital work never completely left Alice. For this reason, and because she wanted to do laboratory work, she decided to specialize in research pathology rather than medical practice. However, her professors suggested that she complete at least one year as an intern for the practical experience. Alice spent two months in Minneapolis at Northwestern Hospital for Women and Children. There she was overworked and shocked by the disregard for proper medical procedures that had been taught in Ann Arbor.

She was once left in charge for three weeks, "alone and unaided." Alice wrote to her cousin Agnes, "Did you ever hear of anything so frightful? Of course, Dr. Hood or Dr.Fifield can be called on at any time, but that does not mean every five minutes, all day, and what shall I do? Even as a matter of time I feel appalled, for every minute almost is taken now, and if I have the nurses' training and the diet kitchen and the admission of patients and accounts and ladies' committees to look after besides, I shall become insane. However, I don't mean to think of it until the time comes. Then I shall pray for no babies."

When an internship opened at the New England Hospital for Women and Children in Boston, Alice eagerly accepted, but she soon wished she were back in Minneapolis. The interns were treated shabbily by the doctors and were set to reading rules and textbooks much of the time. At first, there were not enough patients to go around and there was much squabbling over dividing the work evenly. Alice longed to be busy again, for she felt that at least she had been gaining the clinical experience that was the purpose of an internship.

Alice wrote, ". . . I never thought before that I was tenacious of my own dignity or jealous of my rights, yet here I find myself growing quite red-hot when I am treated--as we all are--like a raw-boned schoolgirl . . . this place makes me feel as if I were tight-laced and must burst my whalebones for a good, long, big breath."

Alice later worked in the hospital's outpatient clinic and it was her first glimpse of how poor people lived. The patients were immigrants who were either unemployed or barely subsisting on sweatshop wages. Alice visited them in the damp basements, stuffy attics, and noisy saloons that were their homes.

When she grieved over a young mother, dead from pneumonia following child-birth, Alice realized she could never develop the emotional detachment she needed to survive as a medical doctor. She renewed her determination to become a research pathologist and, after seeing the devastating effects of poverty, hoped to combine it with social work.

Advanced Pathology Studies

Alice needed more training to establish her career and at that time Germany was home to the foremost experts in advanced pathology studies. Her sister Edith had been awarded a fellowship to study the classics in Germany, so the two left together in the fall of 1895.

Alice studied at the universities in Leipzig and Munich. She was allowed to hear lectures only if she remained in the background, away from male professors and students. Never was she on equal footing with her male peers. The German men were fond of asking repeatedly, "But who will darn the stockings if women are going to be bacteriologists?"

Exasperated by this attitude, Alice wrote in her autobiography, "I had to accept the thinly veiled contempt of many of my teachers and fellow students because I was at once an American and a woman, therefore uneducated and incapable of real study."

Several professors, respected authorities in the

field and with whom Alice had hoped to study, refused to allow her to attend autopsies or perform animal experiments. Bitterly disappointed, Alice claimed that she left Germany with little more knowledge about pathology than she had arrived with.

Raising Awareness at Hull House

When she returned to the United States in 1896, Alice continued her study of pathology at Johns Hopkins Medical School in Baltimore. One year later, she accepted a job as professor of pathology at the Women's Medical College of Northwestern University. Alice was excited not only because it was her first paying position, but it would take her to Chicago, where Jane Addams' Hull House was located.

Hull House, established in 1889, was just one of nearly a hundred such settlement houses in the country. Established in poor neighborhoods, they were run by educated men and women who wished to lead lives of service. Hull House provided free medical care, English classes, a nursery for working mothers, and other opportunities for education.

Working at Hull House exposed Alice to a new level of poverty. She had first seen it in Boston, but in the Chicago slums she lived in the middle of it. The area was a six-mile stretch of factories, tiny, over-crowded cheap wooden houses, garbage and sewage-filled streets, and flocks of hungry immigrant children playing in muddy alleys.

While Alice worked to improve the health of the people who visited Hull House, a terrible suspicion began to form. The stories her patients told her horrified Alice. Steel mill laborers unconscious from breathing carbon monoxide. Stockyard employees with pneumonia and rheumatism. Enamel workers suffering from abdominal pain and paralysis of their wrists, both signs of severe lead poisoning. Slowly Alice became aware these workers were getting sick, becoming disabled, and even dying from their occupations.

In 1907, she stumbled upon the book *Dangerous Trades* by Sir Thomas Oliver. The book was a survey of the industrial hazards in British factories. It supported Alice's own suspicions, and she set out to find the same kind of information about American industry. But every article that she read was about conditions in European countries only. There was no mention of industrial diseases and American workers. Perhaps thinking of her mother's words, "Somebody must do something about it," Alice decided there was nothing else to do but investigate the problem herself.

Investigating Occupational Hazards

Alice kept gathering first-hand stories from workers, but there was no scientific evidence available yet to prove her theories. Even so, in 1908, she published one of the first American articles on the subject. One aspect Alice found distressing was the open denial of the problem by those connected with industry and especially those in the medical community. Most claimed that the standards in American factories were so much higher than their foreign counterparts that the evidence in *Dangerous Trades* couldn't possibly be relevant.

The first real breakthrough came with John Andrews' study of "phossy jaw" in the match industry. Caused by breathing in phosphorus fumes, the disease often resulted in painful facial disfiguration. His investigation covered 150 cases from 15 of the 16 match factories in the United States. Soon after sharing the results with Alice, the report was made public. A French chemist developed a substitute for phosphorus, and in 1912, Congress passed a law which levied a tax on phosphorus matches, which ended their manufacture.

In 1910, Alice was one of five doctors appointed by the state of Illinois to an Occupational Disease Commission. Her job was to survey the hazards of lead poisoning in Illinois factories. In her autobiography, Alice wrote, "It was pioneering, exploration of an unknown field. No young doctor nowadays can hope for work as exciting and rewarding. Everything I discovered was new and most of it was really valuable. I knew nothing of the manufacturing processes, but I learned them on the spot . . .From the first I became convinced that what I must look for was lead dust and lead fumes, that men were poisoned by breathing poisoned air. . ."

Alice investigated factories, interviewed employers, visited hospitals, studied medical records, and interviewed workers in their homes. She uncovered more than seventy manufacturing processes that exposed workers to lead poisoning, including the making of storage batteries and enamel paint.

As a result of the evidence she presented to the Illinois legislature in 1911, they enacted the first occupational disease laws. Employers had to provide financial compensation for employees exposed to industrial dangers. Insurance companies in turn required the factories to enforce new safety measures and provide medical check-ups for employees handling toxic substances.

For the next ten years, Alice worked as a special investigator for the U.S. Bureau of Labor Statistics, for which she received no regular salary. She conducted a national survey of lead poisoning like the one she had done in Illinois. She also investigated the conditions in munitions factories and copper mines. In other industries, Alice studied the toxic effects of carbon monoxide, arsenic, mercury, and radium.

In spite of the opposition that she sometimes met, Alice wrote, "I often feel that my sex is a help, not a handicap. Employers and doctors appear more willing to listen to me as I tell them their duty toward their employees and patients than they would be if I were a man."

A Leading Authority

By 1915, Alice was one of only a handful of industrial disease specialists in the world and she was considered to be the leading American authority on lead poisoning. She published *Industrial Poisons in the United States* in 1925, the first textbook on this topic. This book and *Industrial Toxicology*, published in 1934, were considered to be instrumental in the passage of worker's compensation laws.

Alice was invited to become an assistant professor at Harvard when they decided to offer a course of study in the subject. In her autobiography, Alice wrote, "Harvard had not changed her attitude toward women students in any way, yet here she was putting a woman on the faculty. It seemed incredible at the time, but later on I came to understand it . . . Industrial medicine had become a much more important branch during the war years, but it still had not attracted men, and I was really about the only candidate available."

Alice was the first woman professor at Harvard, but because of her gender, was denied football tickets, was barred from the Faculty Club, and was not allowed to participate in the procession at commencement exercises. And, in spite of her achievements as a doctor and social reformer, she was never promoted to a higher faculty position there simply because she was a woman.

Life After Retirement

At age 65, Alice was forced to retire from Harvard, but she continued working for industrial reform and remained a social activist. She was a consultant for the Division of Labor Standards of the U.S. Department of Labor and was also a member of the health committee of the League of Nations. In 1943, she published her autobiography, *Exploring the Dangerous Trades.*

Alice Hamilton's efforts improved the work environments of millions of workers and gave them legal protection on the job. She was able to reach the goal she had set for herself--being of service to people while using her knowledge of pathology. Alice described her work as " . . . scientific only in part, but human and practical in greater measure."

The recognition Alice's achievements brought her was not the most important thing. It was the knowledge that she had made a difference in the quality of life for the working class. She said, "For me the satisfaction is that things are better now, and I had some part in it."

Alice Hamilton died on September 22, 1970, a few months after her one hundredth birthday.

(Courtesy, Colorado Historical Society;
negative 10029342, Swan Collection)

Chapter Five

Florence Sabin
(1871-1953)
Anatomist

"How glad I am to so affirm my profound faith in the
special fitness of women for the medical profession . . .
no one would now advocate eliminating the work of a
Madame Curie because of a prejudice against
the sex of the worker."
--from an article written in 1922

Florence Sabin, a first-year medical student at Johns
Hopkins University, worked at her lab table, preparing
slides for examination. She was practicing the technique
of using special dyes to stain tissue specimens. Florence
possessed both the patience and the delicate hand required
for the process. The images on her slides, magnified under
the powerful lens of the microscope, emerged sharp and
rich in detail. Her concentration was interrupted by a
young-looking man who quietly asked if he could have a

look. Puzzled, she moved aside, thinking he was a fellow student.

"Nice," was his only comment. Then he stepped back and casually made his way around the room, observing the others. She found out later he was Franklin Paine Mall, a world-renowned anatomist and a professor at Johns Hopkins.

As a teacher, Mall rarely offered verbal praise. He believed that only the most gifted students (a rare one in 10,000 occurrence, according to Mall) were worthy of training in medical research.

Following their first encounter in 1896, Mall demonstrated repeated interest in Florence's exceptional work. He became her mentor, and for the next twenty years, she strived to meet his exacting standards.

One of her most significant achievements was research into the origins of the lymphatic system. It was invaluable to doctors for understanding the workings of the human body. She also studied how the body's immune system fights tuberculosis, a major public health threat of the 1920's.

Following her retirement, she began a new career at the age of 73. She headed a committee charged with cleaning up the chaotic public health system in her home state of Colorado. The Sabin Program reforms led to stricter control of infectious diseases, laws to ensure the purity of milk, and sanitary methods of sewage disposal. Florence Sabin has been called the foremost female medical researcher in the first half of the twentieth century. The magnitude of her contributions to public health and the advancement of women is immeasurable.

~~~~~~~~~~~~~~~~~~~~~~~~

Florence was born on November 9, 1871, in Central City, a Colorado mining town. She was the second daughter of Serena and George Sabin. Her sister Mary was two years older.

Florence's father left Vermont for Colorado in 1860 and found a job as a mining engineer. The Colorado gold rush, which had begun in the 1850's, was still luring treasure seekers to the state. Her mother arrived five years later to take a teaching position, which she gave up when she married.

The family resided in a small house cut into a steep hill. They had no indoor plumbing. Water for drinking and washing was purchased from door-to-door peddlers and stored in barrels. Although living conditions were primitive, Florence and Mary were happy. They wandered freely over the unspoiled landscape, climbing nearby hills, bird-watching, and gathering flowers.

When Florence was four, the family moved to Denver where her father had purchased a small mining company. Her mother was thrilled because the bigger town offered better schools. As a former teacher, education for her daughters was a priority.

In 1877, after a difficult labor, Serena gave birth to a son. Florence was only six years old but helped care for the baby while her mother recovered. She developed a strong attachment to him and was grief-stricken when he died before the year was out.

Serena became pregnant again the following year

without regaining her full strength. She died in childbirth on Florence's seventh birthday. Several weeks later, that newborn son died, too. Sabin was anxious about the welfare of his daughters. They needed his attention, but work kept him away from home for weeks at a time. Reluctantly, he decided to send them to Wolfe Hall, a boarding school in Denver.

Florence and Mary were heartbroken. Still grieving for their mother and little brothers, their misery was compounded by the loss of a normal family life. Florence became hostile towards her father during his infrequent visits. Sabin realized he had made a mistake.

A New Family in Illinois

In 1880, George sent the girls to the home of his brother Albert, who lived with his wife and son near Chicago. Florence and Mary flourished under their warm, nurturing care. Their uncle was a schoolteacher who encouraged them to read books, take music lessons, and study nature.

The girls made summertime visits to their paternal grandparents' Vermont farm. Their grandmother delighted in telling them stories from the Sabin genealogy, especially about ancestors who had been doctors.

Levi Sabin had become the first doctor in the family in 1798. Florence's grandfather had practiced medicine and her father had attended two years of medical school before getting sidetracked by the gold rush.

"Too bad you're not a boy," her grandmother remarked. "You would have made a good doctor." Thinking that it didn't seem fair at all, Florence vowed that she would indeed become a doctor.

Boarding School in Vermont

The sisters left Illinois in 1885 to attend a private boarding school in Vermont. Florence was fourteen and Mary sixteen. The Vermont Academy had an excellent academic reputation.

Florence also further developed her interest in music and devoted all of her spare time to practicing the piano. Abandoning her vow to become a doctor, Florence flirted with the romantic idea of becoming a concert pianist. But when a classmate criticized her ordinary playing, Florence admitted to herself the truth. So she turned to what she loved best after music--science.

Science, she discovered, was her natural gift. Students at the Academy were encouraged to create their own research projects. Florence blossomed in the laboratory and experienced none of the discouragement that piano study had brought her.

She graduated with honors in 1888 and decided to follow her sister Mary to Smith College.

Encouragement to Enter the Medical Field

Smith College was founded because the doors to all-male universities were closed to women. Only thirteen years old when Florence arrived there, it provided a setting in which women could learn on the same level as men.

Her course of study included a heavy concentration in mathematics and zoology.

Florence's hard work and intelligence caught the eye of the school physician, Dr. Grace Preston. Dr. Preston encouraged Florence to consider medicine as a career, noting her excellent grades and precise work in the laboratory.

Dr. Preston was leading the way for female doctors during a time when medical schools were refusing to accept women. However, the status quo was upended with rumors that a new medical school was going to be established at Johns Hopkins University. It was being funded by a group of wealthy women under the condition that women be admitted as well as men.

When Florence heard the news, she was excited but wary about the expense. Dr. Preston assured Florence that if she could scrape together enough money for the first year, aid in the form of scholarships would likely follow.

On a visit home, Florence shared her hopes of becoming a doctor. Her sister warned her against asking for help from their father. His mining company was in financial trouble. Mary was supporting the family by teaching mathematics at Wolfe Hall, the boarding school the sisters had attended years before.

Florence returned to Smith for her senior year still determined to attend medical school. She earned a little money as a tutor, but it wasn't nearly enough. By graduation day in 1893, the same year Johns Hopkins Medical School opened, Florence realized it would be years before she could enroll.

But better later than never, she reasoned. She had patience as well as determination. In order to finance her dream of entering a traditional male field, she turned to a traditional female occupation. Florence became a teacher.

For two years she taught zoology and algebra at Wolfe Hall. She kept expenses at a minimum by living at home and saved most of her salary. Then in the fall of 1895, Smith College asked if she'd be interested in a substitute teaching position for a zoology professor on leave. Florence accepted.

Her classroom instruction showed that she had gift of inspiration as well as a genius for science. Her superior performance at Smith led to the awarding of a fellowship for the summer of 1896.

The fellowship took her to the Marine Biological Laboratories at Woods Hole, Massachusetts. There she assisted several scientists with their laboratory projects and fine-tuned her own microscope skills. She kept back some of the fellowship money. Added to her savings from three years' teaching, it was finally sufficient to cover medical school tuition.

One of the "Hen Medics"

Florence was a member of the fourth class to enter Johns Hopkins Medical School. During its first year, only three of the twenty-two students were women. By the time Florence arrived, a total of sixteen women were enrolled.

In spite of the fact that they were to be on equal footing with the men, the female students had to endure derogatory comments and practical jokes from their male classmates. Women doctors of the time were scornfully referred to as "hen medics," so the women's dormitory there was dubbed "The Hen House."

Florence was not upset or embarrassed by references to the human body, as young ladies were expected to be. She was unshakeable in the face of relentless teasing.

Once, before a lecture on diabetes, a group of male students sent corsages of sweet peas to the women in the class. The "sweet pea" pun--referring to high blood sugar level in urine--did not bring the shocked response they wanted. The tables were turned when the women, with Florence in the lead, wore the corsages to the lecture.

The Influence of Franklin Paine Mall

Franklin Mall, the school's first professor of anatomy, employed unorthodox teaching methods. He eschewed textbooks and lectures. A sign in his laboratory read, "Your Body is Your Textbook." He believed the laboratory should be the arena of scientific discovery and encouraged students to work independently on projects he assigned.

When Florence was a sophomore, Mall assigned her to research the lymphatic system. This system is a vital part of the body's defense against disease and is not fully understood even today. Then it was commonly believed that lymphatics was a system separate from the blood vessels but connected through openings at the lymphatic endings.

Working with lymph vessels from pig embryos and colored dyes, Florence completed meticulous observations with her microscope. After reviewing her carefully prepared slides and notes, she shared her conclusions with Mall.

She suspected that the lymphatic system was not separate after all. It actually budded forth from the blood vessels rather than growing toward the veins. If her research was accurate, her conclusion contradicted the current scientific belief. Mall advised her to conduct the experiments again to verify the results.

During her final year of medical school, Florence began a study of the human brain. Professor Mall provided her with the brain of a newborn infant and from it she made a beeswax model. The model was so stunning in its perfection that Mall had copies of it made in Germany.

Later, the notes and drawings she had amassed from this project were arranged into the book *An Atlas of the Medulla and Midbrain.* Published in 1901, it was the definitive reference book on the brain for the next 30 years.

Choosing Medical Research or Medical Practice

Florence graduated from medical school in 1900 and applied for one of three available internships at the Hopkins Hospital. A problem arose when Florence and a female classmate both were eligible for the position. The hospital board did not want to give two openings to women, leaving only one for a man.

When feminists protested, the hospital backed down. Both women received the internships they deserved. After completing a year-long program, Florence was qualified to apply for a staff position at the hospital.

However, hospital policy forbade the employment of female physicians.

The "Women of Baltimore," the collective name given to the women who had financed the medical school, objected to the policy. But before any action could be taken, Franklin Mall stepped into the melee.

Mall was certain that Florence belonged in a medical laboratory, not in medical practice. She had the potential to become a top-notch research scientist. The "Women" agreed and offered her a fellowship of $900 annually to work with Mall.

It didn't take much more to convince Florence. Working in the lab had always left her with a sense of peace and contentment. Vivid memories of one particular graduation requirement — overseeing the birth of nine babies — still gave her a bad "case of nerves." Yes, she much preferred the quiet of the lab to the chaos of the delivery room.

A Career in Teaching and Research

Florence renewed her lymphatics study, searching for more evidence in support of her theory. When the significance of her research was realized, Johns Hopkins offered her an assistant professorship. This made her the first female faculty member there.

In 1903, the publication of her findings stirred up controversy. But with Mall behind her, she said, "The facts are correct and have been verified, the reasoning was correct and has been justified."

The paper earned Florence a Naples Table

Fellowship. The $1,000 prize enabled her to travel to Europe for further study.

Upon her return to Johns Hopkins, she was promoted to associate professor of anatomy. The $2,500 salary gave her financial independence and, she hoped, job security. Florence believed the "problem" of her gender was no longer a question.

Although Florence was devoted to research, she was equally serious about her teaching. She wrote, "All teachers should be engaged in research. Research lifts teaching to a higher plane."

Just as Mall had done for her, Florence would point out research topics to students and then let them make their own discoveries. As a teacher who continued to engage in scientific research, Florence was an influential role model. Several of her students themselves went on to become well-known researchers.

In 1917, Mall died unexpectedly after an operation for gallstones. Everyone believed that Florence would be appointed to fill his spot as chairman of the anatomy department. But Florence was forced to face the fact that no matter that no matter how impressive were her credentials, the school would not give such an important position to a woman. The job was handed to one of Florence's former students--a man.

Her students were infuriated and planned a demonstration against the trustees' decision. Florence begged them not to cause any trouble publicly.

In private, however, she was heartsick. She struggled to reconcile the school's position with something she had written shortly before: "Women get exactly what they deserve in this world, and needn't think they are discriminated against. They can have whatever they are willing to work for."

Perhaps as a consolation prize, the school asked her to head the histology department. The position was not as prestigious, but it would make her the first woman to achieve full professorship at Johns Hopkins.

Florence chose to accept the injustice with grace and humility. Her work was more important than proving a point or seeking revenge. When asked why she didn't leave Johns Hopkins, she replied, "I have research in progress."

Aiding the Fight for Women's Rights

The laboratory provided Florence some measure of comfort. Even though memories of Mall abounded there, this helped her deal with his death. And by immersing herself in science, she renewed her belief that hard work was the key to unlocking the doors holding women back.

Over the next eight years, Florence earned a solid reputation as a first-rate medical researcher. Her focus turned to the development of blood vessels and blood cells, both closely related to the lymphatic system. From a visit to Germany, she brought back a new non-toxic technique for staining cells. The papers she published garnered the attention of scientists world-wide.

Florence also received several important honors during this period. In 1921, she was selected to introduce Marie Curie to a gathering of the American Association of University Women. At the invitation of the Peking

Medical Union, she traveled to China to present a paper on the origins of blood cells. In 1924, she was named the first woman president of the American Association of Anatomists. Then in 1925, she was voted into the National Academy of Sciences. She was the first woman to gain membership in this prestigious body and would remain the lone female member for the next twenty years.

Although her work absorbed most of her time, Florence felt compelled to be active in the women's movement. She marched in demonstrations and supported the cause for suffrage through letter-writing campaigns.

However, several prominent feminists suggested to her that she was a more valuable asset in the laboratory than on the street. As a woman who had successfully cracked the male hierarchy of medical research, she was an inspiring example. Florence could wage the battle from the inside out---by encouraging women to enter the field of medicine.

A Move to the Rockefeller Institute

Shortly after she was inducted into the Academy, Florence received another honor. This one prompted her to consider leaving Johns Hopkins after a career there spanning a quarter of a century.

Simon Flexner, director of the Rockefeller Institute for Medical Research, offered her a position as a full-time researcher. Flexner was aware of Florence's genius and called her "the most eminent of all living scientists." His instructions by the Institute's board had been to hire only the brightest and most innovative scientists he could find.   There were no restrictions regarding gender.

The Rockefeller Institute, located in New York, had been in operation for only twenty years. In that brief period, it had become one of the leading research centers in the world, known particularly for its study of infectious diseases.

At this time, tuberculosis was the number one cause of death in the United States for people of all ages. Since 1922, the Florence's research had centered on the white blood cells called monocytes. It was believed that monocytes played a role in the body's fight against tuberculosis.

The idea that her work could improve the quality of people's lives appealed to Florence. Even though her lymphatics studies had been important, the prevention of disease seemed more socially relevant and personally satisfying.

In the fall of 1925, Florence packed her research materials and headed to New York. Her absence left a hollow echo in the Johns Hopkins laboratory. As for Florence, she departed with only one regret. She had to leave behind her teaching.

More Honors before Retirement

At the Rockefeller Institute, Florence was named head of the Department of Cellular studies. Her new career began with the study of the pathology of tuberculosis. It later evolved into work with the formation of antibodies, which are produced in response to disease.

In 1926, she joined the research committee of the

National Tuberculosis Association. The members were involved in many groups -- universities, other research institutes, and pharmaceutical companies. The committee's purpose was to consolidate all of the tuberculosis research taking place with the hope of controlling the disease sooner.

Florence published over 50 papers in scientific journals and accumulated more awards. More than a dozen universities bestowed her with honorary degrees. In 1931 she was named by *Good Housekeeping* magazine as one of America's twelve most eminent living women.

She wrote a biography of Franklin Paine Mall which took six years to complete. Published in 1934, it was considered a scientific and literary achievement. She received a $5,000 prize for scientific research in 1935, an award given in honor of M. Carey Thomas, one of the Women of Baltimore. That same year her name was on a list of the country's ten most outstanding women.

In 1938, Florence marked her thirteenth year at the Institute. Still engaged in research at 67 years of age, Florence knew it was time to retire. She unselfishly believed she was standing in the way of younger researchers.

Cleaning up Colorado

Florence returned to Colorado and shared an apartment with her sister Mary. She had too much energy to retire completely. Florence served on the boards of numerous medical organizations and made several trips back to New York for short periods to continue research.

But these many activities left her floundering for lack of a specific focus.

The answer came in 1944 when Governor John Vivian appointed Florence to head a public health committee. He had no real intention of endorsing reform and thus thought the soft-spoken, seventy-three year old lady would not create a stir. How wrong he was!

Florence was appalled by the conditions of the Colorado health system. The laws were antiquated and enforcement was hampered by insufficient funding. She uncovered high tuberculosis rates, livestock infected with brucellosis, infant deaths from diphtheria, contaminated milk, and waterways polluted by improper sewage disposal.

"We think of our state as a health resort, yet we're dying faster than people in most other states," she said.

Florence made public the horrifying statistics and then campaigned her way across the state, lobbying for change. The result was legislation that became known as the Sabin health bills. It took several more years of travel and work to get the laws passed, but Florence persisted. W. Lee Konous, Colorado's new governor, supported her efforts. He described her as "Florence, the atom bomb."

"All Good Things at the Price of Labor"

In 1951, at the age of eighty, Florence retired for good. That year she won the Lasker Award, the highest award given in science. At the University of Colorado, the Sabin Building for Research in Cellular Biology was dedicated in her name.

Two years later, on October 3, 1953, while

watching her favorite baseball team, the Brooklyn Dodgers, play in the World Series, she suffered a fatal heart attack.

Upon her death, Denver mayor Quigg Newton said, "Dr. Sabin was one of the greatest persons I've ever known. She was learned, she was wise, she was humble. She loved the world and every living creature in it."

Florence was honored by her home state when she was one of two people chosen to represent Colorado in Statuary Hall in the U.S. Capitol Building in Washington, D.C. The life-size bronze statue was completed and dedicated in 1959.

Florence Sabin was a pioneer for the advancement of women in medicine and a selfless public servant. She was an example of how to achieve happiness and longevity through work.

A specially designed bookplate made carried the motto she called her "secret" to living. Below a drawing of a microscope was the following inscription: "Thou O God, dost sell unto us all good things at the price of labor." Three years before her death, she told a reporter, " Whether work means digging ditches, driving a car, or working for world understanding, it will keep you healthy and young if you work with enjoyment. It's resistance to work--not work itself--that ages people."

Chapter Six

Alice Catherine Evans
(1881-1975)
Bacteriologist

*"The nineteenth amendment [allowing women to vote]
was not a part of the constitution of the United States
when the controversy began and he was not accustomed
to considering a scientific idea
proposed by a woman."*
--Alice on why a prominent scientist rejected her research

Alice Evans dribbled the basketball with ease as she raced down the court. Leaving the opposing team behind her, she neared the goal and swept the ball up and in. Her teammates cheered this substitute guard who scored whenever she handled the ball.

Eighteen-year-old Alice, exhilarated by the physical activity and the camaraderie, felt proud to be a member of the newly-organized women's team at Susquehanna Collegiate Institute. Basketball provided an outlet for her boundless energy and restless spirit, even if it meant she was dubbed "unladylike." In 1898, it was still considered scandalous for girls to sweat.

But sweat they did, especially since they were covered in black from neck to toe. The players' "jerseys" were long-sleeved, high-necked heavy knit sweaters. The bottom half of their uniform was a pair of baggy, woolen bloomers. Their long hair was piled up in thick masses, crowned with a large bow. Leather high-topped shoes and long black stockings completed the outfit.

Alice's independence and disregard for convention were assets she would use throughout her career. As a researcher at the U.S. Department of Agriculture, she discovered that bovine bacteria in raw milk could infect humans with undulant fever. The disease was known to cause infections of the brain and central nervous system and heart dysfunction.

When Alice advocated pasteurization of milk, she found herself embroiled in a battle of wills with the dairy industry, public health officials, physicians, and some of the most eminent scientists of the day.

Alice persisted in spite of the skepticism and personal attacks. Subsequent studies by other scientists eventually confirmed her findings. By the early 1930's the dairy industry was enforcing mandatory pasteurization.

Her discovery, called "one of the most medically important in the early 20th century," spared thousands of people all over the world from the miseries of the disease.

~~~~~~~~~~~~~~~~~~~~~~~~~~~~~

Alice was born in the small Pennsylvania farm community

of Neath on January 29, 1881. She joined a brother Morgan, almost two years old. Her parents William and Anne were of Welsh ancestry and valued hard work. They also believed that education would give their children (daughters as well as sons) the resources to better their station in life.

When Alice was five and six years old, she was taught at home by her parents. After that, she attended the one-room school house in Neath where she earned outstanding grades. Her lessons at home continued. Her father often read aloud from books and newspapers, initiating family discussions about politics, economics, and religion.

Along with that knowledge came the first inkling that, in spite of equal education, her brother had more career choices.

Training to be a Teacher

Alice was fifteen years old when she completed eighth grade. There was no district high school in Neath, but she planned to attend Susquehanna Collegiate Institute in Towanda, Pennsylvania, where over one thousand young women had been trained as teachers.

For two years, she helped her parents with the farm work. Her mother supplemented their income by selling sewing machines. In 1898, there was enough money for Alice to enroll at SCI.

While she was resigned to the limits placed on her future, she was also eager to return to her studies. However, the coursework failed to challenge Alice. Her quick mind and her home education left her better prepared than most other students.

Luckily, she had a role in the beginnings of women's athletics there. It suited her sense of adventure and probably satisfied her longing for more than what society allowed girls at the time.

In her memoirs, Alice wrote humorously of an incident in which she dislocated a finger playing basketball. The doctor, shaking his head in disapproval, would not set it back in place for her. If she wanted to play basketball she would have to suffer the results, he said.

The finger eventually healed but remained slightly out of joint for the rest of her life. Alice said the crooked finger was "a reminder that if someone oversteps conformity, one is apt to have to pay a price."

Alice earned her teaching certificate in 1901. Like many of the other girls, Alice returned to her hometown and the school where she had once been a student.

The dull routine drove her to distraction and boredom. She missed her friends and the excitement of basketball. Dissatisfied but helpless to escape her situation, she signed her teaching contract year after year.

Rural Teachers Given Opportunity

By the end of her fourth term, Alice desperately wondered how much longer she could continue as "Miss Evans, schoolmarm." An answer to her unspoken plea came from Cornell University in Ithaca, New York.

The college was offering a tuition-free nature study course to rural teachers. The idea was developed by Liberty Hyde Bailey, dean of the College of Agriculture.

He thought the way to instill a love of natural history in young boys and girls from farming areas was to first train their teachers.

Alice could hardly believe her good fortune. In later years she wrote, "Until my academic education was completed, I seemed never to have the opportunity to make a choice in matters concerning my future. I always stepped into the only suitable opening I could see on the horizon."

Looking ahead to the next two years as a welcome respite from teaching, Alice left for New York. She had no tuition worries and the money she had earned teaching would provide living expenses.

A Different Direction at Cornell

Alice devoted her full concentration and energy to the program, not wanting to waste a moment of her time at Cornell. She studied each night long after her housemates had closed their books and dimmed their lights. Alice said, "I had no way of gauging my own ability against the general run of students, so I worked very hard for fear of not measuring up."

Alice studied under some of the most prominent professors at Cornell. Burt G. Wilder taught vertebrate zoology, a core class of the nature study curriculum. He had been at the university since its founding. John Henry Comstock, an entomologist, and his wife, Anna Botsford Comstock, the first woman to hold the rank of professor at Cornell, had been nature study instructors for more than 50 years.

Liberty Hyde Bailey himself was an expert botanist

and traveled all over the world collecting plant samples. Alice called it "an exceptional privilege" to be one of his students.

When the course ended, Alice's upgraded teaching certificate entitled her to a higher salary. But Alice couldn't return to teaching. With a renewed sense of purpose, she dreamed of a career in science. The first step would be earning a bachelor's degree.

Specializing in Bacteriology

In the early 1900's, Cornell University was leading other colleges in agricultural research. As new scientific technology emerged, some areas lacked qualified research scientists. The university attempted to fill in the gap by offering free tuition to students who would specialize in dairying, horticulture, animal husbandry, bacteriology, or other agriculture-related majors.

It was an easy decision for Alice, who loved biology, to choose bacteriology as her specialty. Although she was on scholarship, Alice needed extra income to help meet living expenses. Her part-time jobs included housecleaning and catalogue indexing. In addition, she still devoted many late night hours to studying. Known by her teachers as a student who could quickly grasp complex ideas, Alice continued to earn excellent marks.

Professor W.A. Stocking, teacher of dairy bacteriology, took particular note of her. He had been asked by a colleague to recommend someone for a graduate scholarship in bacteriology at the University of Wisconsin.

Alice applied for the scholarship even though it had never been awarded to a woman. She waited, anxious and uncertain. Would her qualifications be strong enough to merit the scholarship over any male applicants?

The scholarship committee thought so. In the spring of 1909, Alice received a letter of congratulations. Winning the scholarship was an important event, showing her that though the walls of gender inequity were thick, they were not impenetrable.

A few weeks later, Alice packed her bachelor of science degree, along with a few clothes and books, and boarded a train for Madison, Wisconsin.

Earning a Master's Degree

Alice's new advisor, Professor E.G. Hastings, suggested that she build up her background in chemistry, even though her scholarship was for bacteriology. As a result, Alice spent more than half of her time in chemistry classes.

One of these was the chemistry of nutrition taught by Elmer V. McCollum. At that time, he was conducting experiments that eventually led to the discovery of vitamin A. His students were among the first to hear the terminology he created, such as vitamine, fat-soluble A, and water-soluble B.

The two semesters passed quickly and by summer, Alice had earned another degree, an M.S. in bacteriology. Then she had to make a decision. Should she continue her studies for a doctorate or seek employment ?

Professor McCollum urged her to work towards a Ph.D. in chemistry, offering to help her obtain a university fellowship. Alice considered the idea. Staying in school would postpone the problem of finding a job. She was that rare creature of the early 1900's--a female scientist. There was no guarantee that she could find work.

But the last few years of intense study had been taxing. She refused McCollum's offer. Alice told herself there would be other supportive people like her professors, men who judged people according to abilities rather than gender.

Working for the U.S. Department of Agriculture

In 1910, the U.S. Department of Agriculture building in Washington, D.C. was undergoing renovations to provide more space for the large numbers of newly-hired scientists. Until the addition was completed, universities around the country were housing experimental work stations. One of these was located at the University of Wisconsin, headed by Alice's former advisor Professor Hastings.

He offered Alice a research position in the Dairy Division. She spent the next three years as part of team investigating methods to improve cheese-making, an important state product. Although the work was not exciting, Alice was relieved to have found a job so quickly.

In 1913, the new Dairy Division laboratories were finished. Alice moved to the capital city, along with hundreds of other scientists.

Alice herself caused a stir when she arrived at the Dairy Division of the Bureau of Animal Industry. The administrators were not expecting a woman. But they couldn't send her back. As a civil service worker, she was protected by law. Only a serious offense could terminate her employment. So Alice was "in", the first woman scientist to hold a permanent position there.

The Dairy Division was engaged in two primary areas of research. The first was refining the process of manufacturing cheese and butter for improved flavor. The second was investigating the sources of bacterial contamination in milk products. Alice collaborated in several team projects in both areas.

Through this work, Alice became interested in the disease brucellosis and its relationship to fresh, unpasteurized milk. Alice was given the go-ahead to investigate the problem independently. Little did she know that her findings would lead to a bitter controversy that would take over a decade to settle.

Discovering the Twin Microbes

Brucellosis was a debilitating disease, characterized by recurrent high fever, sweating, and joint pain. It was difficult to diagnose accurately, in part because it was thought to actually be several separate diseases: Malta fever, occurring in goats; Bang's disease, in cows; and in humans, undulant fever.

Alice's investigation focused on the organism *Bacillus abortus,* known to cause miscarriage in animals. She pored over reports from studies done between 1910 and 1912. Alice learned that the microbe thrived in infected cows as well as animals that appeared healthy. The reports warned that since the bacteria was found in cow's milk, a threat to human health was likely.

The warnings had gone unheeded. It was generally accepted that the form of the disease found in animals was different from the disease occurring in humans. So the assumption was that the disease could not be passed from an infected animal to a human. Because of her research, Alice took issue with that assumption.

"The idea of drinking milk contaminated with bacteria capable of causing disease in animals was distasteful to me. I wanted to know more about these organisms," Alice said. "Especially, I wanted to know whether they were related to any species known to cause human disease."

When she consulted the head of pathology, he revealed that goat's milk had been found to carry the organism causing human undulant fever. Was there a link between *Bacillus abortus* and *Micrococcus melitensis*, the bacteria found in goats?

Though their scientific names had classified them as different families (*bacillus* meaning rod-shaped and *coccus* meaning oval- or sphere-shaped), the bacteria had to be related, Alice theorized. *B.abortus* and *M. Melitensis* had the same habitat--the udders of animals that appeared to be healthy. Both produced similar symptoms in infected humans and animals.

Over the next four years, through various experiments with an endless parade of bacteria samples, agar cultures, test tubes, and microscopes, Alice found definitive evidence of the answer she was hoping for. The two organisms were related, yes; but even more astounding was the fact they were one and the same.

Facing the Skeptics

Alice presented her findings at the 1917 annual meeting of the Society of American Bacteriologists. She said, "Considering the close relationship between the two organisms, and the reported frequency of virulent strains of *B. abortus* in cow's milk, it would seem remarkable that we do not have a disease resembling Malta fever in this country..."

Alice concluded, "Are we sure that the cases of glandular disease, or cases of abortion, or possibly disease of the respiratory tract may not sometimes occur among human subjects in this country as a result of drinking raw cow's milk?"

No one believed her. Skeptics asked, "If these organisms are closely related, why haven't other bacteriologists seen it?" What they really meant was, "You are a woman and you don't have an advanced degree. How could you find something that men with more education haven't?"

Alice understood the reaction and had even expected it. She remarked, "The whole business of these supposedly different microbes being identical twins was too simple." And Alice knew why other scientists had overlooked it.

They couldn't see past the shapes that supposedly made the germs unrelated. Alice, though, had noted that some of the *M. melitensis* bacteria were actually rodshaped, like the *B. abortus*. When they divided, the rods sometimes looked "shortened," in effect, making them seem spherical.

The criticism left Alice undaunted. But she

postponed further brucellosis research when the spinal meningitis epidemic threatened the United States during World War I.

In Service to Public Health

Alice left the Department of Agriculture and obtained a position at the Hygienic Laboratory (now the National Institutes of Health) in April 1918. She worked with a team of doctors who were trying to improve the antiserum treatment for meningitis.

A few months later when Spanish influenza struck the eastern United States, Alice was assigned to investigating the influenza bacillus. Almost immediately she fell ill herself. By the time she recovered, the influenza epidemic had passed, so she returned to the *meningococci* study.

Meanwhile, controversy over Alice's twin microbe theory grew after it was published in a scientific journal. Despite the personal attacks on her integrity, Alice refused to let bitterness impede her research. She returned to her study of brucellosis.

Alice delved into reports from British and French scientists on Malta fever and any other scientific papers she could find. Several problems came to light.

First, the disease was often mis-diagnosed, particularly if a patient didn't have the undulating fever curve. Such cases were misidentified as typhoid fever, malaria, or tuberculosis.

Second, Dr. David Bruce and his wife, discoverers of the bacillus in goat milk in 1887, mistakenly classified it as *micrococcus*. Bacteriology was a new science at that time and the couple were working with primitive microscopic equipment. But this error led them to believe that it was unrelated to the bacterium found in cow's milk.

Finally, what Alice saw as likely the most important hindrance, was the prevailing public attitude towards milk as a non-carrier of disease. Robert Koch, the German physician respected for his ground-breaking work with tuberculosis, cholera, and rabies, was in part responsible for this attitude.

In 1901, he stated unequivocally that humans could not get tuberculosis by drinking milk from cows infected with the disease. In spite of evidence to the contrary, his view was accepted for several years.

Over a decade before, the U.S. Public Health Service had declared that the only way to prevent milk from being a carrier of communicable diseases was pasteurization. But when the Commission of Milk Standards met in 1910, the guidelines they established did not include pasteurization. They believed the cleanliness standards set by certification were sufficient.

Alice turned her attention to earlier laboratory reports from the Dairy Division and began her own study on milk samples from infected cows. Too many people were getting sick from drinking milk they thought was safe. The law had to be changed.

Continuing the Fight

Dr. Theobald Smith was Alice's most vocal enemy. He published papers in 1919 and 1925 arguing that contaminated milk from infected cows was not a health hazard to humans. When Alice was invited to become a member of the Committee of Infectious Abortion with the National Research Council, he wrote to them questioning the validity of her work.

Alice's dignified response was a letter of her own to Dr. William Welch, who had once asked her to try to resolve her differences with Dr. Smith. She wrote, "It seems to me that Dr. Smith could not take the point of view that the so-called *B. abortus* is non-pathogenic for man if he knew the evidence that has accumulated in the last few months in South Africa as well as this country."

Alice had received reports from Rhodesia of cases of human brucellosis caused by drinking infected cow's milk. In Arizona, an outbreak of undulant fever was attributed to goat's milk. Shortly after, a physician from John Hopkins Hospital sent Alice a bacterial strain for testing. When the sample proved to be *B. abortus*, Alice was ecstatic. It was the first known case of undulant fever in the U.S. in which the trail of infection did not lead directly back to a goat.

In one experiment, Alice injected a pregnant cow with the goat bacteria. After the cow miscarried, the fetus was found to have *M. melitensis* in its tissues. It was also in the milk--further evidence that the two microbes were related.

When one of 500 human blood samples she was analyzing tested positive for *B. abortus*, Alice discovered the patient routinely drank raw cow's milk. Now there were two cases of human brucellosis, caused not by goat bacteria, but pointing to cow's milk as the source of infection.

Alice's position was gaining strength. Soon she

would have enough documentation that there could be no more argument against the need for pasteurization. Alice continued her research in earnest. Ironically, she would soon personally testify to the misery of brucellosis.

Living with Brucellosis

Bacteriologists were aware of the inherent dangers connected with their work. Certainly Alice took precautions when handling the brucellae germs in the laboratory. But at that time scientists were unaware of the air-borne nature of these microbes and their ability to enter the body through the respiratory tract.

The disease struck Alice in 1922. For the next 23 years, between periods of recovery, she suffered episodes ranging from mild attacks to bouts so severe she had to be hospitalized.

In spite of her illness, Alice labored on, always believing the truth would win out. Somehow managing to find humor in her situation, she said, "It seems as if those bugs had a special animosity toward me since I made that discovery."

Slowly but surely, the evidence kept mounting. Awareness of human brucellosis as a disease of bovine origin grew. Hundreds of cases were reported from nine European countries, Palestine, Canada, and the United States. In Denmark, researchers reported 500 cases over a 20-month period.

By the end of the decade, there could be no more doubt. Even the reluctant dairymen were forced to concede the fact that raw milk from infected cattle could transmit the disease to humans. By 1930, most large

American cities were passing laws requiring milk pasteurization.

An Honorable Career

In 1928 Alice was elected the first woman president of the Society of American Biologists (known today as the American Society for Microbiology). She continued her study of chronic brucellosis until 1939, when hypersensitivity to the live cultures forced her to stop.

Alice then took up an investigation of immunity to streptococcal infections. There were 30 known types of streptococci when she began. By her 1945 retirement, 46 types had been identified and sulfa drugs and penicillin had been added in the fight against such diseases.

Following her retirement, Alice became a popular speaker, especially with women's groups. She lectured frequently about women's career development, especially in the sciences. In suggesting that the microscopic sciences were more receptive to women, she was fond of saying, "Devotion to minute details in quiet seclusion does not appeal to most men."

Alice suffered a stroke at the age of 94 and died on September 5, 1975. Her tombstone reads, "The gentle hunter, having pursued and tamed her quarry, crossed over to a new home."

The "gentle hunter" faced her opponents with dignity, grace, and intelligence. Never mind that she was only a woman with no advanced degree. Perhaps the foundation for her strength of character was laid when she first defied convention by playing basketball. For the rest of her life, she stood firm in her convictions.

During one of her lectures, Alice said, "Women have proved that their mental capacity for scientific achievement is equal that of men." Her discovery of the twin microbes and the campaign to make milk safe for human consumption distinguish her as one of the leading scientists of this century.

U.S. Navy Photo

Chapter Seven

Grace Murray Hopper
(1906-1992)
Computer Scientist

*"I'm going to shoot someone for saying that someday.
In the computer industry, with changes coming
as fast as they do, you just can't afford
to have people saying that."*
--Grace's response to "We've always done it that way."

Seven-year-old Grace Murray sat cross-legged on the floor of her parents bedroom holding an alarm clock. She was curious about the ticking and the ringing noises made by the sturdy little clock with the round face, spindly legs, and brass bell on top.With a small screwdriver she had taken from a kitchen drawer, Grace deftly removed the back plate. But before she could see how they were positioned, gears, wheels, and springs tumbled out.

Grace knew she could put them back together if only she could look inside another clock. She ran to one of the other bedrooms in her family's summer home.

When she unscrewed the back of a second clock, again the pieces fell out too quickly.

Not one to give up easily, Grace dismantled five more alarm clocks, with the same result. Grace's mother found her surrounded by seven clock faces and their scattered fragments, still puzzling over how to put them back together. Mary Murray did not reprimand her daughter too severely, for she knew of her daughter's fascination with mechanical gadgets. Mrs. Murray and her husband Walter Murray wholly approved of Grace's interest in things other than tea sets and dolls. She was allowed to explore her natural abilities in math, science, and machines. One of Grace's favorite toys was a construction set called a Structiron kit. She created objects with moveable parts from nuts, bolts, metal pieces, and an electric motor.

Because of her parents' progressive thinking, Grace ultimately found herself tinkering with the most revolutionary machine of this century--the computer.

When others thought writing a standard computer language was impossible, Grace proved them wrong. The development of COBOL--Common Business Oriented Language--was the direct result of her pioneering work in computer programming. It is still one of the most widely used computer languages in the world today.

Grace also helped to create the technology that has made modern computers a reality. Her achievements earned her the titles "Amazing Grace," "Grand Old Lady of Software," and "Grandmother of the Computer Age."

Grace, the oldest of three children, was born on December 9, 1906 into a family who had high expectations for themselves. In fact, she gave credit to this attitude for her accomplishments. She said, "My mother's very great interest in mathematics and my father's, a house full of books, a constant interest in learning, an early interest in reading, and insatiable curiosity ... these were a primary influence all the way along."

Grace's maternal grandfather, John Van Horne, was a New York City surveyor. In the late 1880's, when Grace's mother Mary was a young girl, she often accompanied him on his outings. She would hold the tall red-and-white striped range pole as steadily as she could while he took measurements. (Years later Grace would enjoy the same privilege.)

The relationship between lines, angles, curves, and intersections intrigued young Mary. She wanted to study geometry in school, but girls weren't allowed to take that subject. However, she was permitted to sit in the hall outside the classroom and listen. Perhaps the memory of this experience was partially responsible for Mary's open attitude concerning her daughter's education.

Although a career was out of the question, Mary Murray's mathematics abilities were applied in a practical way when her husband's illness forced her to take over the financial responsibilities. Walter Murray suffered from hardening of the arteries in his legs and they were eventually amputated.

Grace observed first hand that a woman could keep accounts, pay bills, figure taxes, and plan a budget.

Her interest in mathematics came from watching her mother wrestle with numbers and win.

The value of perseverance came from her father. After the loss of his legs, he was fitted with wooden ones. Murray told Grace that if he could learn to walk again, she should be able to do just about anything.

A Rigorous Early Education

Grace was educated in private girls' schools. She skipped two elementary grades and so was sixteen years old when she finished high school. Grace wanted to major in math at Vassar. But when she took the college entrance examination, she failed the Latin section.

Grace did not give up. Instead, she enrolled in a college prep school in New Jersey. Hartridge School required its students to take English, Latin, one other foreign language, and history or science. The girls also had to participate in fine arts activities such as drama and choir and physical activities such as dancing, gymnastics, basketball, and horseback riding.

The next time she took the entrance exam, Grace passed all sections, including Latin. She entered Vassar in the fall of 1924 at the age of eighteen.

Ready for Vassar and Yale

Grace decided to major in math and physics, but she was interested in many subject areas. In addition to her regular classes, she audited beginning science courses such as botany, physiology, and geology. Her eagerness to learn even prompted her to audit classes in business and economics.

Grace's classmates soon found out that she was an excellent teacher. She could take a complicated idea and find a way to physically demonstrate it. During a tutoring session for students failing physics, she wanted to explain the theory of displacement. Dramatically, she dropped one of those students into a tub filled with water. As the others watched the water line rise in proportion to the surprised student's weight, the theory became clear.

During her senior year, Grace was elected to Phi Beta Kappa, an honorary society for the nation's top students. Following her 1928 graduation with a Bachelor's degree, she won a Vassar fellowship which awarded her money to continue her education. She enrolled at Yale and earned a master's degree in 1930. That summer Grace was married to Vincent Foster Hopper.

A Doctorate in Mathematics

The couple settled in New York following European honeymoon. Vincent was an English instructor at New York University's School of Commerce. Grace was offered a teaching position at Vassar with a yearly salary of $800.

Grace gladly accepted. The Great Depression had just begun, leaving many people throughout the country unemployed. Grace was also eager to return to mathematics, and she could do that through teaching.

She first taught algebra, trigonometry, and calculus. Then she developed courses in probability, statistics, and analysis. Just as she had when she was tutoring, Grace continued to use novel methods of instruction. Her classroom projects inspired her students and helped them understand mathematics as more than abstract concepts.

Grace loved teaching almost as much as she loved learning. So while maintaining a rigorous schedule at Vassar, she began studying for her Ph.D. at Yale.

At that time, fewer than ten students at the school were working towards a doctorate in mathematics. Grace was one of four women. After her graduation in 1934, only seven doctorates in mathematics were awarded over the next three years.

Even today, it is rare for a woman to earn a Ph.D. in mathematics. Given these statistics, Grace's accomplishment was nothing less than remarkable.

Joining the Navy

When the Japanese bombed Pearl Harbor on December 7, 1941, the United States entered World War II. Grace, like millions of other patriotic Americans, wanted to support her country. Men volunteered or were drafted into the armed services. Other men and women worked in defense factories producing airplanes, ships, tanks, and guns.

Grace said, "Everyone joined something," and she wanted to join the Navy. Her maternal great-grandfather had been a rear admiral in the Navy. And, Grace jokingly explained, "I love the color blue!"

During the first part of the war, however, women were not being accepted into the Navy. But a severe shortage of sailors developed as thousands of men were lost to injury or death in the Pacific. So Congress established the WAVES (Women Accepted for Voluntary Emergency Service). These women would replace the men working in naval offices in the United States. The men could then be sent overseas.

Recruiting posters proclaimed, "Enlist in the WAVES. Release a man to fight at sea." But when Grace went to sign up, she was turned away. First of all, they said, at age 36, she was too old. Secondly, she was too small. A woman of Grace's height, five feet six inches, was supposed to weigh at least 121 pounds. At 105 pounds, Grace was 16 pounds underweight.

Most importantly, "mathematics professor" was an occupation classified by the government as vital to the war effort. People working in these jobs were encouraged to remain civilians, where it was believed they could best serve their country.

Somehow Grace obtained waivers to bypass the age and weight requirements. Then she talked Vassar into giving her a leave of absence from her teaching position. No longer employed in a classified occupation, Grace was sworn in as a member of the Women's Reserve of the United States Naval Reserve in December 1943.

Midshipman's School at Smith College in Massachusetts followed. The other 500 officer trainees were "youngsters" to Grace. They were the same age as her students back at Vassar.

Grace thrived on the rigors of military life. She marched and did calisthenics. She learned to identify American, British, and German aircraft. She learned the difference between a carrier and a submarine. She studied naval history and customs.

And Grace loved wearing that blue uniform. She said it saved her from the bother of deciding what to wear in the morning.

Grace graduated at the top of her class in June 1944. Upon her commission as a lieutenant junior grade, she visited the cemetery where her great grandfather was buried. Placing flowers on his grave, Grace assured him that "it was all right for females to be Navy officers."

Meeting Her First Computer

The Navy sent Grace to Harvard University and the Bureau of Ordnance Computation Project. The military needed information to help them launch and fire modern weapons more accurately. Mathematicians like Grace were to develop formulas and instructions for programming the Mark I computer to do the calculations for firing tables.

The Mark I looked nothing like the personal computers of today. It stood eight feet high and extended for 51 feet along the wall of the basement laboratory. Weighing in at five tons, the computer had over 800,000 parts connected by 500 miles of wire.

Through the glass frame the electro mechanical relay switches could be seen, and thousands of tiny lights blinked off and on. Clacking noises were made from machines that recorded information. Grace, who had once been fascinated by the parts of a simple alarm clock, looked in awe at the monster machine. She said, "It was the fanciest gadget I'd ever seen. I had to find out how it worked."

Computer programming at that time involved

several steps. After the proper formula was identified, it had to be rewritten as numerical instructions. Then those numbers had to be changed into binary code, which uses only two digits: 0 and 1. Finally, the binary code was "punched" into rolls of paper tape that were fed into the computer. The computer "read" the pattern of holes as commands.

The team working on programming the Mark I included Grace and seven others --three officers and four enlisted men. As the wartime conflict intensified, so did the demand for weapons information.

Grace said, "All of a sudden we had self-propelled rockets, and we had to compute where they were going and what they were going to do. The development of the atomic bomb also required a tremendous amount of computation, as did acoustic and magnetic mines."

The team kept the Mark I running twenty-four hours a day. In case the computer stopped working overnight, they took turns sleeping at their desks. Through trial and error, they learned shortcuts to speed up the process of coding, translating, and punching the commands.

Howard Aiken, commander of bureau operations, felt that all programmers should benefit from the shortcuts his team developed. He suggested that Grace write a book. When she protested, he sternly responded, "You're in the Navy now." Grace had no choice but to write the book. Titled *A Manual of Operation for the Automatic Sequence Controlled Calculator*, it was published by Harvard University Press in 1946.

Grace and her colleagues began the construction

of the Mark II computer in the summer of 1945. It was five times faster than the Mark I and was the first multiprocessor, capable of running two programs at once.

One evening, the Mark II abruptly stopped running. After checking several relay switches, Grace discovered a moth had been smashed between two of them. It had interrupted electrical contact and shut down the computer. Using a pair of tweezers, Grace removed the insect. On a whim, she taped it into the logbook and humorously remarked, "I've debugged the computer." Thus Grace coined the term "computer bug" which is now part of our everyday computer lingo.

When the war was over, Grace and her husband were divorced. They had no children nor had they lived together for several years. In 1946, she was forced to retire from active duty. Grace was 40 years old, too old, according to the Navy. However, she did remain a member of the Naval Reserve.

Grace's wartime leave of absence from Vassar became permanent. She was having too much fun with computers to go back to being a mathematics professor.

Creating UNIVAC I

Grace stayed on at Harvard for three more years. Then in 1949, she accepted a position with the Eckert-Mauchly Computer Corporation. She took a risk by leaving Harvard, but the risk was characteristic of her nature.

The company's vision for the future was what Grace herself foresaw: computers being used by workers in factories, business, and sales. That philosophy was nonexistent among her Harvard colleagues who believed only scientists could understand and run computers.

But in 1951, Eckert-Mauchley revolutionized the computer industry with the creation of the UNIVAC I. It was the first mass-produced commercial computer and the smallest ever built. It was a mere 14 feet long and used vacuum tubes instead of relay switches. It could process 3,000 additions and subtractions per second. Besides speed, its greatest asset was that it had internal memory. Instructions could be stored inside of the computer on magnetic tape instead of on punch cards or paper tape.

Grace, as senior mathematician, was instrumental in the development of UNIVAC I. She realized that failure was a very real possibility and that many people were waiting for it to happen. As usual, Grace's sense of humor carried her through.

In describing her team's attitude, she explained, "We used to say that if UNIVAC I didn't work, we were going to throw it out one side of the factory, which was a junkyard, and we were going to jump out the other side, which was a cemetery."

While the UNIVAC I was a huge success, Grace thought it presented one more challenge. She thought it was possible to create sets of instructions, called subroutines, that could be coded and called up many times. Thus the computer could perform repeated functions without being given step-by-step instructions each time. This meant that the computer would have to recognize codes in one language and then translate them to call up the subroutines.

Grace's colleagues told her this was impossible.

This only made Grace more determined. She envisioned a program that would "let the computer do the work . . . [it would] call the pieces and put them together."

The Need for a Universal Computer Language

By 1952, Grace had devised a system which she named the A-0 compiler (A for algebraic). It provided a set of instructions that would translate mathematical code into machine code. The code could be read and understood by the computer, which would then perform the required calculations. Grace explained, "All I had to do was to write down a set of call numbers, let the computer find them on the tape, bring them over and do the additions."

Unbelievably, it was two years before other programmers accepted the fact that her compiler worked. "I had a running compiler and nobody would touch it because, they carefully told me, computers could only do arithmetic; they could not do programs," Grace said.

Grace believed there was a way to write computer programs using the English language. Again her skeptics scoffed at the idea. When she was told outright that she could never do it, she stubbornly made up her mind that she would.

Grace had come to realize that a language barrier kept business people from using computers. Common mathematical words like logarithm, sine, and cosine were foreign to them. They needed a program that used business accounting jargon--inventory, cash flow, and assets.

By 1955, Grace had written a code of twenty

commands that included add, subtract, divide, multiply, move, replace, and count. She called the new compiler the B-0 (B for business). It was renamed Flowmatic because, Grace said, "...those doggone salespeople wanted a fancier name."

Flowmatic was a huge leap for programmers. It was the first language that permitted English words for both the operating data and the instructions for calculations.

Flowmatic made it possible to integrate computers into business. Insurance companies used them to estimate policy costs, inventory managers used them to track purchases, and many companies used them to store information.

Soon business people started asking for specific programs to help them perform tasks particular to their type of business. They wanted to manage their company's information through data processing. So different programmers designed language-based programs to meet the needs of these companies. By 1957, there were three major computer languages used by American companies and numerous others were developed as well.

But an enormous problem soon emerged. There was no one language which could be understood by all programmers or used interchangeably on any computer. Grace said, "We lost our language in mathematics--a well-known, universal language, as easily understood here as in Tokyo or Berlin." She continued trying to convince others of the urgent need for a universal computer language.

In 1959, a panel of computer experts met to discuss the creation of a universal language. The result was COBOL (**CO**mmon **B**usiness **O**riented **L**anguage) which was largely based on Flowmatic. Grace was not directly involved in writing COBOL, but she did act as technical adviser.

In 1962, it was accepted as the common programming language in the United States and the world. COBOL made computers user-friendly and enabled businesses to handle large amounts of information efficiently.

A Short-Lived Retirement

In 1966, after being promoted to the rank of commander, Grace was asked to retire from the Naval Reserve. She was sixty years old. Grace had served twenty-three years, longer than the twenty years allowed to reservists. Her retirement became effective on December 31, 1996, which she described as "the saddest day of my life."

Only seven months later, Grace received a phone call from Navy officials, asking her to return to temporary duty. There were problems with COBOL and no one could solve them. Grace agreed to the challenge. She said, "I came running--I always do when the Navy sends for me."

Grace's assignment was to standardize COBOL and promote its use throughout the Navy. Her official job title was Director of Navy Programming Languages Group. She was given an office in the Pentagon and a small staff. They produced and published a training manual called *Fundamentals of COBOL.*

Her temporary duty turned into twenty more years

of service to the Navy. Grace achieved the rank of rear admiral in 1985, the first woman to do so. One year later, at the age of 79, she retired for good. For the rest of her life, Grace would say, "I have received many awards and many honors. But I have already received the highest award I will ever receive--the privilege and responsibility of serving in the United States Navy."

A Teacher to the End

Following her retirement, Grace was hired by Digital Equipment Corporation as a senior consultant. She also maintained a busy speaking schedule, sometimes with four or five engagements per week. "I don't think I will ever be able to really retire," she said. "I'm not content being a spectator." It gave her the opportunity to do the two things she enjoyed the most--teaching and getting people excited about computers.

During her speeches, she used anecdotes and concrete examples to illustrate her points. For example, in demonstrating what a nanosecond was, she would hand out 11.8 inch long wires to audiences. This was the distance electricity could travel in one-billionth of a second--a nanosecond.

Grace encouraged innovative ideas and the acceptance of change. A favorite saying of hers was, "Go ahead and do it. You can apologize later." She also frequently used this navy analogy: "A ship in port is safe. But that's not what ships are for. Be good ships. Sail out to sea, and do new things."

On her office wall was a clock whose numerals ran backwards from 12, instead of forwards from 1. The hands also turned counterclockwise. Grace said, "It tells perfectly good time. The first day people have trouble reading it. By the third day, they realize there is no real reason for the clock to run clockwise."

Her unconventional outlook on life and work fueled a career that was remarkable for its achievements and longevity. In 1969, she was named Computer Science Man of the Year. In 1973, she became the first American and the first woman to be named a Distinguished Fellow of the British Computer Society.

When Grace was inducted into the Engineering and Science Hall of Fame in 1984, she was put into the company of George Washington Carver, Jonas Salk, and Thomas Edison. In 1991, she was awarded the National Medal of Technology, the first woman to receive it.

Grace once said she wanted to live at least until age 94. She wanted to be around for the New Year's celebration on December 31, 1999. And, she said, "I want to point back to the early days of the computer and say to all the doubters, 'See? We told you the computer could do all that!'"

But Grace died on January 1, 1992. She was eighty-five years old. Even though she didn't live to see the first part of her wish fulfilled, the second part of her wish has come true.

Thanks to Grace, personal computers are as commonplace as the automobile. It is reasonable to imagine that, without her vision of user-friendly computers for everyone, those machines today could be found only on the desks of scientists and computer specialists.

But because Grace Murray Hopper refused to accept the premise "It can't be done," millions of people all over the world use computers every day for work and play.

© The Nobel Foundation

Chapter Eight

Gertrude Belle Elion
(1918-1999)
Chemist

*"It's the most rewarding form of life there is. I started
at a time when women didn't go into science, when it
was difficult enough for men to get a job, and even less
likely for women. Quite frankly, it was the war that
opened the door to women in science. Suddenly, there
was a need for people and the men were gone."*
--commenting on finding a job in a laboratory

Gertrude Elion was already up and getting dressed for
work when her telephone rang. It was 6:30 am on October
17, 1988. She picked up the phone and an unfamiliar voice
greeted her with, "Congratulations! You've won the
Nobel Prize in medicine." Gertrude was certain it was a
prank call. "Quit your kidding," she told him. "I don't
think it's funny."

"No, really it's true," insisted the reporter on the other end.

"Well, I haven't heard anything about it. How do you know about it?" she asked.

The reporter told her that a press release from Stockholm had been made public at noon in Sweeden, which was 6:00 am New York time.

"You are a co-recipient with your colleague Dr. George Hitchings and Sir James Black of London," he said. Still not convinced, Gertrude hung up the phone. But it immediately began ringing again. It was another reporter. Gertrude finally believed the news when she received a telegram from the Nobel Committee the next day.

Gertrude explained the delay. "They had been trying to reach me by phone, but it was constantly occupied. So that's how I found out." The rest of the day was hectic. She said, "I never finished dressing, because there was a reporter at the door from a local newspaper, and I'm trying to answer the phone, and trying to comb my hair, and the photographer is taking pictures, and some of those pictures are really weird!"

Gertrude was asked many times if winning a Nobel Prize was the highlight of her career. She insisted that it was not. What if the focus of a person's life was only to win an award and the award never came?

For her, the reward of living a life of scientific research was curing patients.

"There's nothing that gives you a lift like seeing somebody get better from a serious disease. The Nobel is something that is going to disappear in a few days. The other [seeing patients recover] is permanent," she said.

During her 40-year career in the pharmaceutical industry, she sought to develop drugs that would bring an end to cancer, leukemia, herpes, and AIDS.

"While blazing new trails as a woman scientist in what was then a man's world, Dr. Elion persevered in work that led to advances in treatments for a variety of diseases," said Robert A. Ingram, chief executive of Glaxo Wellcome, the company for which Gertrude worked. "[Her] love of science was surpassed only by her compassion for people."

~~~~~~~~~~~~~~~~~~~~~~~~

Gertrude Belle Elion was born on January 13, 1918 in New York City to Jewish immigrant parents. Her father Robert, a dentist, had come from Lithuania. Her mother Bertha, a housewife, was from Russia. Gertrude had one brother Herbert, who was born when she was six years old.

Gertrude was a bright little girl who skipped several grades. Thus she completed high school at age fifteen. It was expected that she would attend college.

"Among immigrant Jews, their one way to success was education, and they all wanted their children to be educated. Furthermore, it's Jewish tradition. The person you admired most was the person with the most education. And particularly because I was the firstborn, and I loved school, and I was good in school, it was obvious that I should go on with my education," Gertrude explained.

Gertrude's ambition to have a career was largely influenced by her mother. "She was always very supportive," Gertrude said, " at a time when many women of her generation would not have been."

Bertha Elion had married at 19 and had no higher education herself. She wanted her daughter to have what she didn't have: a career outside the home and the freedom to spend her own money any way she chose.

The summer after high school graduation, Gertrude watched her grandfather die painfully from stomach cancer. This led to a determination to be a research scientist because, she said, "Nobody should have to suffer that much."

No one, neither family nor teachers, had ever actively discouraged her from pursuing a career in science, although her father would have liked her to enter his field, dentistry. The accomplishments of Marie Curie made her believe that a woman could achieve in science. But Gertrude was equally inspired by stories of other scientists. In high school she had read *Microbe Hunters* by Paul Dekruif. It covered not only the discoveries made by scientists such as Jenner and Pasteur, but their lives as well. She said, "That book gave me the feeling that it was all right to struggle, it was all right for it to be hard. It didn't have to come easily, yet there were so many things to be done in science."

Gertrude was already facing a difficult situation. Her family had been in financial trouble since the stock market crash in 1929. There was no money to send her to college. Her only prospect was Hunter College, a city university that did not charge tuition. There were many more applicants than openings, but Gertrude was accepted because of her excellent grades.

She chose chemistry as her field of study because she had disliked the animal dissections required in her high school biology class. Four years later, at age nineteen, Gertrude earned her degree, graduating summa cum laude.

Overcoming Discrimination and Discouragement

Following her graduation from college, Gertrude still aspired to do cancer research. She knew this would require an advanced degree. Since she had no means to pay the tuition, she tried to obtain a graduate assistantship. When fifteen fellowship applications for graduate study were turned down and her hunt for a job was unsuccessful, Gertrude began to realize what she had so naively ignored before: it was 1937 and she was a woman.

The Depression had left many men unemployed, so jobs were scarce to begin with. But even when a job was open, Gertrude discovered it was open only to men.

During one interview she was told, "You're qualified. But we've never had a woman in the laboratory before, and we think you'd be a distracting influence."

Gertrude gave up. But she had to earn a living in some way, so she tried a traditional female path, secretarial school. She hated it. " I knew that I couldn't--I wouldn't--ever stay there. It was only six weeks, which was about as much as I could take."

Fortunately, Gertrude was offered a three-month position teaching biochemistry to nursing students. She took the job and happily left secretarial school behind. The teaching job, which paid a grand total of $200, was followed by a job working for an organic chemist she had met at a party. He was unable to pay her, but at that point, Gertrude didn't care. She would be in a laboratory at last, getting the experience she needed to reach her goal of becoming a research scientist. She stayed a year and a half and was eventually paid $20 a week.

She used that money for graduate school, where she was the only woman in her chemistry classes. Even with a master's degree, there were still no laboratory positions open to her. So, working as a permanent substitute, Gertrude taught high school chemistry and physics for two years.

It was around this time that Gertrude met the man she hoped she would marry. Leonard was a bright young student of statistics and had won a fellowship abroad. Upon his return, however, he developed a serious bacterial infection in the valves and lining of his heart. The infection was one easily cured today by modern antibiotics, but Leonard died because the discovery of penicillin was five years away.

Gertrude never fully recovered from the shock of losing him and his death affected both her personal life and her career as a scientist. She never married, even though her family continued to hope she would. She told subsequent would-be suitors that she didn't have time for marriage. Instead, she immersed herself in her work.

This personal tragedy emphasized what she had already learned from her grand-father's death. Discovering new drugs was critical to saving human lives. It was a lesson she was forced to face a third time when, in 1956, her mother developed cervical cancer and died. This increased her resolve to research and create life-saving drugs.

WWII Opens Laboratory Doors

A turning point for Gertrude came in 1942. Employers abandoned discrimination in the rush to fill jobs vacated by the men who left to serve in World War II. Companies had no alternative but to give women a chance if they wanted to stay in business. Gertrude left her teaching position when she was offered work in the industrial laboratory of the A&P grocery chain.

As a food analyst, Gertrude tested the quality and the traits such as acidity, color, and texture of foods such as pickles, fruit, and mayonnaise. It wasn't exactly what she had in mind, but she was back in the laboratory. And even though it wasn't cancer research, she was learning about new scientific instrumentations and techniques.

By 1944, she decided if she was ever going to get into a research lab, she had to seize an opportunity before all the men returned home from the war. Besides, the work had become repetitive and Gertrude felt that she had learned as much as she could.

Johnson & Johnson laboratories had recently made a corporate decision to enter the pharmaceutical industry. Gertrude was one of two people hired to assist the head chemist. Six months later, the company reversed its decision to begin drug research. She was offered a new job, measuring the tensile strength of sutures. Gertrude turned them down. She wasn't interested in that kind of work, even though it meant she was unemployed once again.

She wasn't out of work for long. By a combination of pure luck and coincidence, Gertrude discovered the existence of the company which was to be her employer for the next 40 years.

Burroughs Wellcome

It was Gertrude's father who put her on the trail of Burroughs Wellcome. He had received some of the company's pharmaceutical samples at his dental office. He encouraged her to contact them. Gertrude was skeptical, but made the call, inquiring whether or not they even had a research laboratory. To her surprise, they did and she was invited for an interview.

George Hitchings, who became her research partner and with whom she would, many years later, share the Nobel Prize, interviewed Gertrude and offered her the job, against the advice of his assistant, Elvira Falco. Gertrude had thought it was promising when she saw another woman. She found out later that Falco, after one look at Elion's striking red hair, perky hat, and elegant suit, had decided she was not laboratory material.

However, Hitchings overruled Falco. He liked the spirited way Gertrude presented herself and was impressed with her academic record. He gave her the job for $50 a week, a substantial increase from her first laboratory job.

She was lucky to have arrived at Burroughs Wellcome when she did. Their policy on drug research was well ahead of other pharmaceutical companies.

Established as a research organization, rather than just a money-making enterprise, the company fed its profits back into research, particularly towards finding drugs to treat serious diseases.

To Gertrude, the opportunity to work at a company like Burroughs Wellcome was the fulfillment of a dream. Finally, she was in a research laboratory where she might discover a cure for cancer, the most important reason behind her drive to become a research scientist.

Also, the scientists themselves were given a lot of freedom. Gertrude called it "enlightened research management." No one was looking over their shoulders, asking questions about what the researchers were doing or what they hadn't done.

And then there was the presence of George Hitchings. The fact that he hired a woman, who was only twenty-six years old and without a Ph.D., was never seriously questioned. He had earned a reputation and respect for doing things differently and looking at things differently. His view proved to be a distinct advantage for both Gertrude and the company.

Hitchings was revolutionizing the way drug research was done. Scientists had been using the trial and error method, which looked at a disease and then randomly tried using different drugs as cures for that disease. He believed that a more rational, systematic approach would work better. Hitchings and his staff did research on the chemicals before the diseases, rather than the other way around.

Years later, she said, "In a sense, I think of it now as invention of new compounds and then discovering what they were good for. . . the compounds themselves ended up being tools for discovery as well as ends in themselves. One of the most important things about discovering new drugs is to let the drug lead you to the answer that nature is trying to hide from you."

Work Becomes Her Life

Gertrude loved her work from the very beginning. She was fascinated by the mystery inherent in the compounds she had been assigned to work with. These were called purines, which scientists felt might be the answer to cancer treatment.

Gertrude worked with an intensity that many believed was not possible for a woman. Even Falco, her female co-worker, was amazed at her ability to maintain focus on a problem. Falco gave her a back-handed compliment when she compared Gertrude's perseverance to that of a man's.

Gertrude was trying to earn her doctorate at this time. While working full-time at Burroughs-Wellcome by day, at night she was traveling three times a week to Brooklyn's Polytechnic Institute. By following this demanding schedule, Gertrude estimated she would have her degree in ten years.

After two years, however, she was confronted by the dean of the school, who insisted she become a full-time student. He accused her of not being serious enough about the Ph.D. Gertrude refused, since it would mean giving up her job. As disappointing as it was to give up her goal of earning a doctorate, she later said, "It was just the wrong time for me to drop my job, and it had been too difficult to find the right kind of job."

Hitchings supported her decision, and had in fact, encouraged her to stay. He told her she could do the work without the doctorate.

"It was very daring. I never questioned him about it. I think he thought there was a certain gleam and a certain intensity in my work. It would take me a little longer perhaps, without a Ph.D., but he was prepared to give me the opportunity. That's what made the difference. Not everyone would have done that."

Gertrude did have some doubt whether she could get along without the Ph.D., but she eventually realized that Hitchings had been right. Gertrude saw that she could learn more by being in the laboratory than earning a degree.

"The amount of work that I put into it was greater than the amount I might have put into my studies at school," she said. "There was nothing to distract me. I could work ten hours a day, seven days a week with no problem. I could work in the lab as long as I wanted. I always took work home. It was my life, it wasn't just my job."

A Major Breakthrough

Gertrude continued creating purine compounds and studying their effects. In 1950, she discovered that one of her purine chemicals could interrupt the development of leukemia cells. It wasn't a cure, but a treatment that could slow down the disease. The drug was 6-mercaptopurine (6-MP) and marketed as Purinethol.

That same year, she also synthesized another drug, one closely related to Purinethol, called Thioguanine. Eventually, both drugs were used in combination with other drugs to successfully treat childhood leukemia. Today, Purinethol is still used for the same purpose, while Thioguanine is used in treating adult leukemia.

Over the next eighteen years, Gertrude worked to make 6-mercaptopurine better. Her responsibilities increased and she began to lead research teams of her own. The compound allopurinol was developed and used to treat gout and to alleviate the unpleasant side effects of chemotherapy.

Her continued research led to a sophisticated derivative of 6-MP called azathriopine, more commonly known as Imuran. It effectively blocked a body's rejection of foreign tissues and thus made organ transplants possible. The majority of the 100,000 kidney transplant patients in the United States since 1962 have benefited from this drug.

Developing Anti-viral Drugs

In 1967, Hitchings retired from active research and Gertrude was named head of the Department of Experimental Therapy. She had become one of the highest-ranking women in the entire pharmaceutical industry.

Her team began research in an area that other pharmaceutical companies had left untouched--drugs to treat viruses. It was accepted scientific belief that any compound strong enough to suppress viral activity would also be extremely toxic to human life and thereby useless as a treatment.

Over the next decade, the team tested and studied various compounds, experimenting with removing sugar molecules from purines to fool and confuse viral enzymes. The result was acyclovir, a drug marketed as Zovirax, the first effective treatment for herpes, shingles, and Epstein-Barr virus. The development of the drug was a landmark in anti-viral research because it showed that different viruses had their own particular enzymes.

Their research eventually led to the development in 1985 of AZT, the first successful treatment of the AIDS virus and the only such drug in the U.S. until 1991. By then Gertrude had retired, but was still working as a consultant. While she is often given credit for the drug, Gertrude said, "The only thing I can claim is training people in the methodology.....The work is all theirs."

Winning the Nobel Prize

Winning the Nobel Prize in 1988 was a huge surprise for both Elion and Hitchings. Hitchings had always believed if he were to win the prize, it would have come ten or fifteen years earlier. It was very unusual for the winners to be given the award for a lifetime body of work, as Hitchings and Elion were. Normally, the Nobel is given earlier in life and for some kind of major discovery.

Gertrude never expected to win at all because, as she later explained, she had three strikes against her. First, she was a woman. Second, very few Nobel Prizes in medicine were given to people working in industry.

Finally, Gertrude did not have a doctoral degree.

However, win they did. In its announcement of the award, the Nobel Committee said, "While drug development had earlier been built on chemical modification of natural products, they introduced a more rational approach based on the understanding of basic biochemical and physiological processes."

Life After the Nobel

Even though she was officially retired, Gertrude Elion's science career continued. Instead of being directly involved in research, she began to teach others. She was a medical research professor at Duke University in Durham, North Carolina, and an adjunct professor of pharmacology at the University of North Carolina, located at Chapel Hill.

She once said, "Science is the kind of discipline where you keep learning all the time. I always wanted a job where you didn't stop learning and there was always something new."

Educating and working with students of all ages became an important focus for her. She said, "Children are very impressionable, they are very curious. You've got to take advantage of that curiosity, to let them realize that there is a big world out there they can discover. If you don't do it when they are young, you are not going to get them back again."

Her commitment to passing on a love for science to young people never wavered. In 1999, two junior high girls from Omaha, Nebraska, selected Gertrude and her inventions as a topic for a school project. They called the pharmaceutical company for information and Gertrude wrote back to them personally, even giving them her phone number. When they decided to fly to North Carolina to interview her, she enthusiastically made arrangements to meet them and give them a tour of her office.

Sadly, a few days before the trip, on February 21, Gertrude died. Her assistant encouraged the girls to come anyway. When they arrived, information packets Gertrude had prepared were on her desk, waiting for them.

Gertrude Belle Elion was 81 years old when she died, but she had continued to work past her 1983 retirement from Burroughs Wellcome. The dedication she showed towards her life's work is an example of what a difference a science career can make in the lives of people everywhere. She owned the patents to 45 drugs, and, although she never earned a Ph.D., she was awarded 25 honorary doctorates.

In 1991, Gertrude was presented the national Medal of Science by President George Bush. That same year she became the first woman elected to the National Inventor's Hall of Fame.

Gertrude understood the connection between what scientists do in the laboratory and the lives of people outside the lab. She said, "I think I'm most proud of the fact that so many of the drugs have really been useful in saving lives."

To Gertrude Belle Elion, what mattered was helping people; there was no greater satisfaction. The lesson learned from the deaths of her grandfather, fiancée, and mother never let her lose sight of the human side of science.

Afterword

All eight women portrayed in this book are exemplary role models for young people today. They exhibited determination, intelligence, patience, and a simple love for their work. These qualities are key to a successful career, no matter what the field.

These women made it clear that they were not looking for rewards or recognition. The drive to succeed was fueled by the thought that they were helping others. This has been the case for many women throughout history. The mere fact of being born female placed women into positions of servitude--as mothers, daughters, wives, teachers, nurses, and social workers.

For these women scientists, the fight for an education and the right to make use of it elevated that position of servitude. Each one's devotion to practicing her particular branch of science was an example of selfless service. They labored not for personal gain but for the benefit of their fellow human beings.

The quotations below are a final look at the struggles, achievements, and words of encouragement that their lives have to offer.

"The science hierarchy at that time was very strict. There was pure science, applied science, and social science. Through chemistry, Swallow tried to bridge all three, and the man in science didn't like it at all."

--biographer Robert Clarke about
Ellen Swallow Richard

"[She was] not only the best of women investigators, but one whose work will hold its own with any of the men of the same degree of advancement."

--E.B. Wilson in a letter about
Nettie Maria Stevens

"It is an anomaly that, though she is recognized the world over as the greatest living expert in this line of work, and her services to the Observatory are so important, yet she holds no official position in the university."

--in 1911, a visiting Committee to the
Harvard Observatory about Annie J. Cannon

"You see, I simply cannot believe that I am a person of more than ordinary ability, though I know that chance has given me a more than ordinary life."

--Alice Hamilton

"The great joy and pleasure she derived from her work was like a contagion among those around her."

--a Rockefeller Institute associate
about Florence Sabin

Bibliography

Bailey, Martha J. *American Women in Science: A Biographical Dictionary.* Santa Barbara: ABC-CLIO, Inc., 1994.

Bartholomew, Rebecca. *Lost Heroines.* West Valley, Utah: Unitah Springs Press, 1997.

Billings, Charlene W. *Grace Hopper: Navy Admiral and Computer Pioneer.* Hillside, N.J.: Enslow, 1989.

Burns, Virginia Law. *Gentle Hunter: A Biography of Alice C. Evans, Bacteriologist.* Laingsburg MI: Enterprise Press, 1993.

Bursztynski, Sue. *Potions to Pulsars: Women Doing Science.* Chicago: Allen & Unwin, 1995.

Camp, Carole Ann. *American Astronomers: Searchers and Wonderers.* Springfield, NJ: Enslow, 1996.

Clarke, Robert C. *Ellen Swallow: The Woman Who Founded Ecology.* Chicago: Follett Publishing Company, 1973.

Cooney, Miriam P. *Celebrating Women in Mathematics and Science*. Reston, VA: National Council of Teachers of Mathematics, 1996.

Epstein, Vivian S. *History of Women in Science for Young People*. VSE Publications, 1994.

Grant, Madeline P. *Alice Hamilton: Pioneer Doctor in Industrial Medicine*. New York: Abeldard Schuman,1967

Hamilton, Alice. *Exploring the Dangerous Trades: The Autobiography of AliceHamilton*. Chicago: Northeastern University Press, 1985.

Kronstadt, Janet. *Florence Sabin: Medical Researcher*. New York: Chelsea House,1990.

MacDonald, Anne L. *Feminine Ingenuity*. New York: Ballantine Books, 1992.

McGrayne, Sharon Bertsch. *Nobel Prize Women in Science: Their Lives, Struggles, and Momentous Discoveries*. Seacaucus, NJ: Birch Lane Press, 1998.

McPherson, Stephanie S. *The Worker's Detective: A Story About Dr. Alice Hamilton.* Minneapolis: Carolrhoda Books, 1992

O'Hern, Elizabeth M. *Profiles of Pioneer Women Scientists*. Washington, DC: Acropolis Books, 1985.

Rossiter, Margaret W. *Women Scientists Before Affirmative Action 1940-1972*. Baltimore: John Hopkins University Press, 1995.

St. Pierre, Stephanie. *Gertrude Elion: Master Chemist*. Vero Beach, FL: RourkeEnterprises, 1993.

Sicherman, Barbara. *Alice Hamilton: A Life in Letters*. Harvard University Press, 1984.

Simonis, Doris, ed. *Lives and Legacies: An Encyclopedia of People Who Changed the World -Scientists, Mathematicians, and Inventors*. Oryx Press, 1999

Stille, Darlene R. *Extraordinary Women of Medicine*. Chicago: Children's Press, 1997.

Stille, Darlene R. *Extraordinary Women Scientists*. Chicago: Children's Press, 1995.

Vare, Ethlie Ann. *Adventurous Spirit: A Story About Ellen Swallow Richards*. Minneapolis: Carolrhoda Books, 1992.

Vare, Ethlie Ann. *Mothers of Invention*. New York: Morrow, 1988.

Varnell, Jeanne. *Women of Consequence: The Colorado Women's Hall of Fame*. Boulder, CO: Johnston Printing, 1999.

Veglahn, Nancy. *Women Scientists*. New York: Facts on File, 1991.

Weatherford, Doris. *American Women's History*. New York: Prentice Hall, 1994.

Whitelaw, Nancy. *Grace Hopper: Programming Pioneer*. New York: W.H. Freeman, 1995.

Young, Lisa. *Contemporary Women Scientists*. New York: Facts on File, 1994.

Internet Sources

Alice Catherine Evans.
<http://www.netsrq.com/~dbois/evans-a.html>

The Alice C. Evans Award.
<http://www.asmusa.org/acasrc/aca7.htm>

Alice Hamilton.
<http://www.netsrq.com/~dbois/hamilton-a.html>

Annie Jump Cannon.
<http://astr.ua.edu/4000ws/CANNON.htm>

Annie Jump Cannon.
<http://www.netsrq.com/~dbois/cannon.html>

Annie Jump Cannon Homepage.
<http://www.astro.wellesley.edu/annie/history.html>

Annie Jump Cannon: Life After the Henry Draper Catalogue. <http://www.aas.org/ publications/ publications/baas/v25n2/aas182/abshmtl.S8103.html>

Annie Jump Cannon: Theorist of Star Spectra. <http://www.sdsc.edu/ScienceWomen/cannon.html>

Autobiography of Gertrude B .Elion. <http://www.nobel.se/laureates/medicine-1988-2-autobio.html>

Biography- Annie Cannon. <http://www.physcis/gmu.edu/classinfo/astr103/CourseNotes/ETCText/Bios/Cannon.htm>

Celebrating 125 Years of MIT Women. <http://alumweb.mit.edu/groups/amita/esr/swallow.html>

The Contributions of Women to the United States Naval Observatory: The Early Years. <http://maia.usno.navy.mil/women_history/moreintro.html>

Creative Quotations from Ellen Swallow Richards. <http://www.bemorecreative.com/one/1481.htm>

Editorial: A Remarkable Life (Gertrude Elion). <http:www.news-observer.com/daily/1999/02/24/edit00.html>

Ellen H. Swallow Richards.
<http://www.scry.com/ayer/health/4417279.HTM>
Ellen Swallow Richards.
<http://www.astr/ua.edu/4000WS/RICHARDS.html>

Ellen Swallow Richards.
<http://www.cals.ncsu.edu/agexed/aee501.esrichards.htm
l>

Ellen Swallow
Richards.<http://www.curie.che.Virginia.EDU:80/scienti
st/richards.html>

Ellen Swallow Richards House--NRHP Travel Itinerary.
<http://www.cr.nps.gov/nr/travel/pwwmh/ma67.htm>

Engines of Our Ingenuity: Episode No. 649-Gertrude
Elion. <http://www.uh.edu/admin/engines/epi649.htm>

Feisty Sabin sought to improve states' health.
http://insidedenver.com/millenium/1026mile.shtml>

Gertrude B. Elion. <http://www-invent-
org.nforce.com/book/book-text/39.html>

Gertrude Elion.
<http://inventorsmuseum.com/GertrudeElion.htm>

Gertrude B. Elion, Nobel Prize Winner and Glaxo
Wellcome Scientist Emeritus, 1918-1999 (Obituary).
<http://www.invent.org/pr22299.html>

Gertrude B. Elion; Nobel-Winning Scientist (Obituary). <http://www.latimes.com:80/ excite/990223/t000016760.html>

Gertrude B. Elion, Obituary. <http://www.rjriley.com/inventors/Elion/obituary.html>

Grace Hopper. <http://www.csn.naples.fl.us/csn/comp-sci-proj/comp-tech-proj-1997-12/97f%>

Grace Hopper. <http://www.whatis.com/gracehop.htm>

Grace Hopper. <http://www.wic.org/ghopper.htm>

Grace Hopper. <http://www.inventorsmuseum.com/GraceHopper.htm>

Grace Murray Hopper. <http://www.cs.yale.edu/homes/tap/Files/hopper-story.html>

The Hall of Science and Exploration: Gertrude B. Elion (profile, biography, and interview). <http://www.achievement.org/autodoc/page/eli0pro-1>

Hidden Histories: Vassar Women in Science. <http://depts.vassar.edu/~anthro/bianco/ hidden/hidden.html>

History of Women in Astronomy: Annie Cannon.
<http://cannon.sfsu.edu~gmarcy/cswa/history/cannon.ht
ml>

Honoring Drug Discoverers.
<http://www.boston.com/globe/search/stories/nobel/1988
/1988j.html>

The Lemelson-MIT Prize Program: Gertrude B. Elion.
<http://web.mit.edu/invent/www/inventorsA-
H/elion.html>

The National Women's Hall of Fame.
<http://www.greatwomen.org>

Nettie Maria Stevens.
<http://www.mbl.edu/html/WOMEN/stevens.html>

Nobelist Enters Hall of Fame.
<http://www.boston.com/globe/search/stories/nobel/1991
/1991s.html>

A Science Odyssey: People and Discoveries: Drugs
Developed for Leukemia.
<http://www.pbs.org/wgbh/aso/databank/entries/dm50le.
html>

Scientific American: Explorations: Women in Science:
Gertrude B.
Elion.<http://www.sciam.com/explorations/1998/042798
women/elion.html>

The Teacher's Corner--Human Inheritance.
<http://biocrs.biomed.brown.edu/Books/
Chapters/Ch%207/Ch7-teachers.html>

Three Share Nobel for Medicine.
<http://www.boston.com/globe/search/stories/nobel/
1988/1988i.html>

Vassar College: Matthew Vassar Founder.
<http://www.vassar.edu/on_matthew.html>

Vermont's Women of Science.
<http://www.vtc.vsc.edu/wit/science.htm

The Wit and Wisdom of Grace Hopper.
<http://ww.cs.yale.edu/homes/tap/Files/
Hopper-wit.html>

Women in Science Scholars Program
<http://www.glaxowellcome.com>

Index